BOTHAM DOWN UNDER

The 1982/3 England–Australia
Test Series

Books by Ian Botham

Botham's Choice (with Kenneth Gregory)

BOTHAM DOWN UNDER

The 1982/3 England-Australia Test Series

IAN BOTHAM

with

IAN JARRETT

COLLINS
8 Grafton Street, London W1
1983

William Collins Sons and Co. Ltd
London · Glasgow · Sydney · Auckland
Toronto · Johannesburg

Botham, Ian
Botham down under.
1. Cricket—Australia   2. Cricket—England
I. Title   II. Jarrett, Ian
796.35′865   GV928.A8

ISBN 0 00 216491 4

Photoset in Linotron Ehrhardt by
Rowland Phototypesetting Ltd
Bury St Edmunds, Suffolk
Made and printed in Great Britain by
Robert Hartnoll Ltd, Bodmin

CONTENTS

ILLUSTRATIONS

1

A Red Arrow Day

I WAS STANDING ALONE in the middle of the empty Taunton cricket ground, scanning the Somerset skies. It was Thursday, 9th September 1982, close to the end of a summer which had been plump with achievement and satisfaction: the Indians had been seen off without too much trouble over three Tests; the Pakistanis – Imran Khan and all – had been pipped in a thrilling finish at Headingley: and now Somerset had destroyed Worcestershire by an innings in two days.

The rest of the Somerset team were no doubt mischievously questioning my motives as I brooded about the pitch, my eyes not moving from the heavens. Perhaps they thought I was seeking divine inspiration for next season. Or maybe it was a late reaction to an incident a few days earlier when a man had pushed me fully-clothed into the deep end of a Bristol night club swimming pool. I couldn't hear the jokes in the dressing-room and didn't care. I knew why I was there and in the next few minutes so did most of the population of Taunton. Suddenly, from behind clouds, four Hawk jet trainers from RAF Kemble in Gloucestershire charged across the Quantock Hills, dipping their wings as they overflew the ground. The Red Arrows, the world-famous aerial acrobats, were saying hello to 'Guy the Gorilla'. I waved back, the hair on the back of my head prickling as emotion lifted me into the clouds. With the scream of jets in my ears, the thrill was as good as scoring a Test hundred, or taking five wickets in an innings at Lord's. They banked across town and returned for a final salute; my jellied legs felt weaker than they ever had on a cricket pitch. Later in life possibly I might struggle to remember some of my Test innings, but I'll never forget the day the Red Arrows came to town. Their gesture was a kind of passing out ceremony for me: three days before I had been kitted out in green flying suit, white gloves and a red and white helmet to join them in high-level loops above the county ground at Taunton. I didn't let on to the waiting photographers that before my first sortie there had been problems with my G-suit, and an early morning breakfast had made a sudden re-appearance. I planned to treat the Red Arrows to a little low-level testing by inviting them to pre-season net practice at Taunton, where I rather fancied some would be less happy with both feet planted on the ground and Joe Garner coming at them from twenty-two paces.

If the trip with the Red Arrows had been a highlight of my summer, there were plenty of other occasions which had lifted my spirits too. In between scoring 208 against India at the Oval, then striking the fastest century of the summer in 52 minutes against Warwickshire, I had kept myself pretty busy ... too busy as far as my wife, Kathy, and even Somerset Cricket Club, were concerned. I had fished for salmon, hacked around golf courses, bought and backed racehorses and crashed two new 140mph Saab Turbo cars during a frightening afternoon on the Thruxton race circuit in Hampshire. After the second spill, which damaged a £12,000 car, I emerged from the twisted metal with the blood of a passenger, thankfully not seriously hurt, dripping down the side of my face. Still, within an hour I was ready to go again, not realizing that I was driving into a difficult situation.

My Somerset club were among those who criticized me for going on to the race circuit. Of course I appreciated their concern that one of their most valuable assets might write himself off permanently, but throughout my life my determination has been always to take part, to squeeze the most out of every day. Too many people would like to see me just sitting on a river bank with a rod in my hand, or warming my carpet slippers by the fire. But I don't want to be in a position in ten years' time where I regret not having tried my hand at different things – then it will be too late to do anything about most of them. I like to think that my approach to life is open and honest; if from time to time I push myself, and the people around me, to the brink, it's from a desire to come out on top. I believe if you are born with a talent, any talent, you should try to exploit it as naturally as possible and not wait for Old Father Time to sneak away with it. I hope the captains I have played under will remember most of all my will-to-win in the team, because that dominates my thoughts more than any personal glory or any new line in the record books. Records have never concerned me; they only add to the pressure if you know about them beforehand. I would like to think I have never turned my back on a challenge, never shirked from taking the ball in a tight situation. Rather, I relish the need to go full-stretch at life, at the game, and when some have frowned at the bravado of it all I hope my performances may speak for me. Nothing gives me greater pride than pulling on an England sweater and being part of a winning England team – let no-one forget that when I'm being criticized for trying to lead my life at a million miles an hour and pointed at for irresponsibility.

Thoughts of the injustice of England's defeat in India the previous winter were at the front of my mind at the start of summer 1982. I believed the better team had not won then, so the double hundred in the Third Test at the Oval gave me immense pleasure, the more so when one cricket writer and former player described it as the best display of attacking strokeplay he had ever seen. The record had been put straight in my own mind. The only result of the series had come in the First Cornhill Test at Lord's when Nottinghamshire's Derek Randall, who had not played for England since January 1980, hit a marvellous 126. Randall had made an offbeat re-entry on the international stage. He had checked in at the Westmoreland Hotel near Lord's on the eve of the match, then departed for a few drinks with friends after the team dinner. Returning, he asked the hotel receptionist for his room key and tripped off up to bed. Or so he thought – the room was full of someone else's belongings. Back at the reception desk a porter eventually whispered in his ear that perhaps he was in the wrong hotel. Sure enough, Derek had gone back to the hotel where England used to stay when he was last in the side; that took a little living down.

Victory against India, though, was merely the appetizer for the major battle of the summer, the three Tests against Imran Khan's Pakistan. It was a series played without much humour and the umpires were under considerable pressure from the players. Abdul Qadir, the little mystery man, gave a wonderful exhibition of the lost art of leg spin in between what appeared to be auditions for the Whitehall Theatre farces. In the first Test at Edgbaston England won comfortably, even though we were nine wickets down in the second innings and only 233 runs ahead. Bob Willis and Bob Taylor got stuck in with useful runs and when I dismissed Mudassar for nought for the second time Pakistan disappeared from the match. Once again it seemed that although Pakistan had a great side in theory, they were struggling to come good when it mattered. Part of the trouble, I'm sure, is that they have always been too quick to find excuses for shortcomings; if they could accept defeat without moaning they would be better prepared to put things right in the next match. At Edgbaston, Javed Miandad claimed a slip catch off David Gower and then kicked the ball away in frustration when the appeal was turned down. His fielding concentration must have suffered. Photographs later showed that the ball had touched the ground. I feel that had an England player reacted in that manner he might not have played again for his country for some considerable time. Even, perhaps especially, in the heat of the moment, it should be remembered that playing for one's country is an honour to be cherished, not abused. Lax standards on the pitch can only encourage comparable spectator behaviour.

For Pakistan the problem was welding eleven players into an effective team, while for England it was not only a problem to win this series, but to find men to take on Australia in the winter. Randall didn't look altogether happy as an opener; Allan Lamb's first steps into Test cricket were slightly shaky ones; and still the difficulty remained of finding young fast bowlers with the pace to disturb players of real quality. There seemed to be plenty of pretenders about but few who looked the part at international level. England were crying out for a young Dennis Lillee but the selectors seemed to be of the opinion that the tried and trusted old guard were best. The loss of the banned South African 'rebels' left a gap not easily filled and Imran Khan hoisted the warning signs as Pakistan levelled the series at Lord's thanks to Mohsin's magnificent double century against an England attack missing Bob Willis, and to the not inconsiderable contribution of Mudassar, whose amazing return of 6 for 32 sliced through England's second innings. At the end of the match, Mohsin bent down and kissed the Lord's turf as Imran said his piece: 'England must do something about its makeshift opening batsmen because I can't see Derek Randall prospering in that position for long.' He added, 'Chris Tavaré gets on the front too readily and it is difficult to see how he will cope with the extra bounce in Australia.'

As the selection for the tour grew closer, the early build-up to our Ashes tour was already coming out of Australia. Kim Hughes, much too dismissively, I thought, pronounced that England were Ian Botham and ten others; in Brisbane Greg Chappell, between building up his business empire, was hoping to take back the captaincy from Hughes. The Ashes temperature was rising, nowhere more noticeably than at Headingley as several players knew they had only one more match in which to book themselves a tour ticket. The selectors dropped Randall to No. 7 in the order, where he always looks more relaxed by his own fidgety standards. Lancashire's left-handed Graeme Fowler, partnering Tavaré in his Test debut, must have had it in his mind that a good performance would make it difficult for the selectors to ignore him for Australia. Sure enough, Graeme made 86 in our second innings and was already soaking himself in the bath, perhaps dreaming of Melbourne and Sydney, when the series moved towards a marvellous climax. For once in my life I rejected a challenge when we were just 29 runs short of victory with 4 wickets to fall: I turned on my heel and walked when umpires Barrie Meyer and David Constant invited us to go off for bad light, an offer I had rejected twice before. But with 5 England wickets falling for 21 runs in 7 overs, my partner Vic Marks and I decided that this wasn't the time for heroics: we would make camp for the night and leave our final onslaught for the morning. At least, that was the plan as we headed back for dinner at the team hotel with wives and girlfriends. For a time Vic stood alone at the bar, smoking and cracking jokes with all the black humour of a prisoner on Death Row. 'Both's told me I haven't got to worry. He's going to finish the match with five 6s.' Chris Tavaré and I joined Vic after dinner and some of the wives relieved the tension by mounting a soda syphon attack on the players. The bookmakers also reckoned that we were going to make something of a splash, quoting us 3-1 on favourites with 100-1 the tie, although they had not counted on me edging a slip catch to Majid when we were still 20 runs short of victory. 'I just knew Ian would get out,' Willis beamed afterwards; but I didn't notice much of a smile on his face when I walked back into the dressing-room to watch the agonizingly drawn-out forty-minute climax on television.

It seemed we needed more like 200 than 20 runs for victory; when we finally made it with 3 wickets to spare reaction exploded like a champagne cork. The skipper had an egg cracked over his head and milk poured down his back – several of us needed two or three showers before we were clean enough to leave the ground. At one stage, Mike Gatting tossed a pair of champagne soaked trousers out of the window with an invitation for someone to take them away. Perhaps the Middlesex batsman knew something the others didn't, for when the tour party for Australia was announced only Gatting of the Headingley team was not included.

Under skipper Bob Willis, the selectors settled on the following squad: David Gower (Leicestershire), Geoff Cook (Northants), Norman Cowans (Middlesex),Graeme Fowler (Lancashire), Ian Gould (Sussex), Eddie Hemmings (Notts), Robin Jackman (Surrey), Allan Lamb (North-ants), Vic Marks (Somerset), Geoff Miller (Derbyshire), Derek Pringle (Essex), Derek Randall (Notts), Chris Tavaré (Kent), Bob Taylor (Derbyshire) and myself. Hampshire's Trevor Jesty later joined the party in Melbourne but didn't appear in any of the Test matches.

In my view we were not a team of world-beaters but perhaps the party had enough talent to present the Australians with some problems. I thought that for us to have a chance of winning the series a couple of the untried players would have to make a significant impact at Test level – not an easy thing to do – and most of the 'old timers' would have to maintain their best form over a lengthy period. At the top of the order, Fowler's place had been cemented on the strength of one innings but now he was going into territory which would for him be fairly alien. He would be battling for a Test place with Geoff Cook, who had been fluttering around the Test side for a couple of seasons without ever presenting an irresist-ible case for inclusion. Now, with Graham Gooch banned from Test cricket for his South African activities, Cook would get an opportunity to fill the gap. The other worry for the touring party surrounded the back-up bowling to the skipper and myself. Bob's knee injuries had been well chronicled over the past seasons; I had suffered a troublesome back which had caused a tightening of the stomach muscles, not permitting me to feel as loose as I would have liked. It was important, then, that the support bowlers should come through on this trip and although Norman Cowans had made a great impression on me with his pace in the match against Middlesex at Weston, he would have to work a lot harder for his successes

With David Gower, inspecting some decidedly 'morning after' stumps.

Dennis Lillee, disturbing the peace again, but David Gower was given not out and went on to score 72.

David Hookes hitting the ball strongly for Australia during the First Test; and the David Gower quickstep.

Sending one down.

in Australia. How big was his heart? How firm was his will? The next few months would tell. Derek Pringle was another who needed to bridge the class gap between university cricket and the Test arena; if he could settle down quickly, there was sure to be a crucial role for him on the tour.

I took myself off to my favourite Scottish salmon river for two weeks – interrupted only by a helicopter trip to play in a Viv Richards benefit golf match – while others worked hard at my tour preparation. In Worcestershire Duncan Fearnley was personally making sure that my bats were to exact specification. I like my bat to weigh around 2 lb 14 oz; when I put three grips on the handle, they add another 3 oz. The aim is for a bat with a mammoth amount of wood on it, which means thick edges and a hump back. I planned to take four bats with me, two of them newly pressed, including my favourite which I had used during the double hundred against India at The Oval; the little crack at the bottom of the blade was repaired in time for me to use it in my opening game of the tour. I knew that if I failed in Australia I couldn't blame the equipment I was carrying with me or lack of help prior to departing. While the batmaker was at work, others were sorting out engagements in a packed diary, answering a vast amount of mail and among hundreds of requests last summer, one was for the boot which I had to have cut open to ease the pain of a damaged toe – autographed, of course.

At home in Epworth, Kathy was a marvellous back-up, happy that this time the whole family would be renting a house in Sydney for a couple of months of the tour. It wasn't too long ago that wives were discouraged from joining tours abroad and there are those who still believe they should leave their husbands to concentrate on the cricket. My view is that some cricket administrators, in their great wisdom and pursuit of the dollar, have turned Test tours into endurance trials and the players, therefore, should be allowed a few home comforts to compensate for this frenzied lifestyle. I can't believe that in Sydney my play suffered because I returned to my wife and family every night instead of being cooped up in the team hotel. I can't believe, either, that there was resentment on the part of other players just because I went back to home-made steak and kidney pie rather than the hotel room service menu.

On 3 October the scene as we gathered in the Lord's indoor school before leaving for Australia was one of good-natured bustle. A trace of nervousness from some, a touch of mature indifference from others who had seen it all before. It was like the first day back at school after the summer holidays and I fancied that even those who were not making their first trip were feeling the excitement. Mike Brearley, in the role of much-loved headmaster, came along to wish us well, hoping perhaps that some of his success Down Under would rub off on this party. Tavaré sat on a bench, swinging his legs and maybe thinking of the first bouncer he would receive from Dennis Lillee. Randall whistled, signed bats and constantly swept his eyes back and forth across the room, exchanging smiles to release the tension. Marks looked serious; Pringle – minus his turquoise leather tie – tried to joke; and Cowans, the new boy, avoided everyone who wanted to talk about his reputation as a prolific eater. 'This is the moment when your selection for the tour really hits home,' he said, really speaking for us all. Bob Willis, striding and staring in that well-known manner of his, reeled off tour titbits for the assembled journalists. 'Botham is now a front-line batsman,' he stressed. 'As such, he must not be bowled into the ground. The trouble will be getting him to let go of the ball. I'll just have to take his sweater down to him at fine leg – or, better still, send someone else down with it.' I posed with the others, then stayed in front of the cameras for some advertising work, accepted silver trophies, agreed to countless interviews and gave my own forecast for the months ahead: 'I know that better touring sides have left this country, but I feel we have the sort of players who will react positively in tight situations.' The knowledge that my family would be joining me in Australia helped to ease the journey to Heathrow to catch the evening Qantas QF2 flight, destination Brisbane.

Four days before a ball had been bowled on tour, one Australian newspaper columnist dismissed our party as dull, faceless men who would send Australia to sleep. Their line of attack seemed to indicate a belief that by poking fun at England they could paper over the arguments surrounding the Australian captaincy. 'The sight of Willis pounding in like some demented chook is enough to send a man to the bar,' said one writer, who was probably already there when he filed copy. Gower was the man 'with the Shirley Temple curls' and Tavaré was the arch-snail who put cobwebs on the television set. Wicketkeeper Bob Taylor didn't escape either: 'But at least Taylor's presence is a surprise for us Australians.

Most of us didn't know that he was alive, let alone still his country's keeper.'

We read it all and laughed; and by the time I ran in to bowl the first ball of the tour to Queensland's former Springbok Kepler Wessels, we were ready to make our reply.

2

The First Test, Perth

I'M A COUNTRY BOY by birth, and many of my happiest cricket memories
are set in the pastoral beauty of the English countryside. School days in
Yeovil were happy and exhilarating; then, as my cricket began to mature, I
experienced the city elegance of Lord's, my college of learning, and a little
later the open, sunny ovals of Taunton, Bath and Weston-super-Mare. As
I progressed there came sterner tasks in more formidable settings –
Edgbaston, Old Trafford and Headingley.

One learned to take the rough with the smooth. There was a fair
amount of rough on the recent winter visits to the West Indies and India,
both enchanting countries for the relaxing holidaymaker but always we
had to be on guard and 'careful what you say'. The tours were scarred by
political manoeuvres and strange umpiring decisions, sometimes to the
accompaniment of fruit-and-veg barrages. These things didn't happen in
Australia, I always believed. There the natives would be warm and
friendly – until you beat them or ruffled their feathers – and there the sun
would shine brightly and reflect its early light in the Swan River, where the
city of Perth stands. Now, the real stuff was to begin. Now, Friday 12
November 1982, would be the start of a life-and-death struggle for an urn
of wood-ash and that struggle would shift from Perth to Brisbane,
Adelaide, Melbourne and Sydney before the final crow of victory was
heard.

Funny, though, that I couldn't get steamed up and jittery at the
prospect. Psychiatrists don't bother knocking at my door – only the rest of
Australia does! On tour, my room is never quiet, even on those rare
occasions when the phone doesn't ring or an England colleague doesn't
drop by for a chat. That Friday morning, I felt more relaxed and lazier

than usual, as I awoke and reached out to switch on my favourite local radio station in Perth, 6KY. Pop music exploded from the speakers of a flash portable stereo set I had bought in one mad, extravagant moment and soon, from a tenth-floor window of the Sheraton Hotel, I was taking in the panorama view of Perth. It is a really beautiful city, with its white sails, stunning river views and haughty black swans.

We had been there for a week, four days of which had been taken up by the match with Western Australia; but there had been a fair amount of spare time in which to appreciate the genuine warmth of the Australian people. There had been a lot of cricket talk and a good few beers to cope with, but that's the way they are out there. It's no good trying to run and hide from it – you're better off trading verbal blow for blow. In any case, I think we all felt we owed the public something after the ear-bashing the television people had been delivering in their build-up to the Test series. Some of the team were a bit apprehensive about the effect this advertising would have, thinking it might induce a hate war between the two sides, with more than the usual number of 'verbals' and bumpers being exchanged on the field.

In the event, scenes worse than anybody could have imagined were to take place in this fateful match at the WACA ground. Could they be put down to the persistent goading of the 'Poms' in the television commercials? Certainly they had no effect on our lads – you've got to have a thick enough skin to cope with all that nonsense when you are picked to play for England in Australia. Most of it I found laughable and puerile, but since some of it was directed at me personally I felt sorry that some of the cash spent on the campaign might not have been used in other ways. But were the television commercials in some measure responsible for the crowd riots? We shall come back to that in a little while.

There were a few problems facing England now that we had completed the four matches running up to the First Test. None was unexpected. The question of opening batsmen was still with us, but we all knew that it was asking a lot and expecting too much for Tavaré, Cook and Fowler to perform right away in the manner of Gooch, Boycott and Larkins. And then there was the problem of strike bowlers. The choice of a gamble at the very outset, and the largely defensive bowling of Robin Jackman, were surely not what we would be looking for at the first stage of a Test series. Attack must be the strategy, I thought, but the initial form of our young openers, both batting and bowling, had, frankly, been depressing and even Bob Willis, a great morale-booster and dressing-room lecturer, was beginning to show the odd worry line. We saw the signs of things to come in the very first match, against Queensland at Brisbane, and although defeat by a substantial margin of 171 runs was not the end of the world – after all, we were still finding our land legs and feeling the pace of the Australian wickets – two centuries by Greg Chappell and Kepler Wessels quickly brought home to us the magnitude of our task over the next two and a half months. Fortunately, the experienced 'old hands' of the England team all hit form quickly. Allan Lamb and David Gower both got hundreds, Geoff Miller showed good control with bat and ball, and Bob Taylor proved he had not lost his secret of eternal youth in breaking the world record number of wicketkeeping victims. All this meant that we could concentrate on the two major problems.

The name of Cowans had cropped up frequently during the early meetings of the selection committee, which consisted of Doug Insole, Norman Gifford, Bob Willis, David Gower and myself. I think we all agreed from the start that young Norman had to be nursed along carefully. Bob's own international baptism had followed a similar pattern some twelve years earlier, so he had the personal experience and knowledge of what goes on in the raw youngster's mind on first meeting Australian pitches and people and the whole vast set-up. It was natural for Bob to become Norman's mentor from the start. He talked to him a lot, and spent a good deal of spare time coaxing and coaching in the nets. He was nursed through the Queensland match, and when he took the wraps off in the next game at Newcastle he had figures of 4 for 46 and 3 for 30 against Northern New South Wales. Not the sternest opposition, agreed – but it was the psychological boost to Norman's morale which mattered at that stage. Eddie Hemmings hit the target as well in this game, picking up 9 wickets cheaply, and with Chris Tavaré celebrating his twenty-eighth birthday with a score of 157 (including a straight 6!), there was a feeling that we could be in for a good tour. All we needed now, as Stanley Holloway might have sung, was 'a little bit of bloomin' luck'.

Bob Willis was under the weather for our third tour match with South Australia at Adelaide, and I skippered the side in a high-scoring draw that told us very little we didn't already know. Miller, Lamb and Randall were still in good nick with the bat, but I was struggling a bit with my batting and bowling and, like Graeme Fowler, my luck seemed to be completely out. Fowler had my sympathy; nothing seemed to go right. He was desperate for runs, only to be run out when the bowler deflected a drive by Tavaré. At least I got a better break in an incident in which I was originally given out, then reinstated. I had swept Chris Harms, the Australian off-spinner, and had accidentally obstructed Kevin Wright from taking a catch. The umpire said 'out', but their skipper David Hookes withdrew the appeal. It was a nice gesture from David, even though I shouldn't have been given out in the first place. I had a feeling we were going to be seeing a lot more of Mr Hookes before this tour was out. A left-hander, he had played a good deal of club cricket in England for Dulwich, and developed into a mighty hitter of the ball. He scored a good-looking 74 for South Australia in their first innings, and only a week earlier had murdered the Victoria attack for the fastest century in Sheffield Shield history. David batted just 43 minutes and faced 35 balls!

The final match before the First Test at Perth, against Western Australia on the Test square, was a vital one for a number of us – Pringle, who had bowled well at times with rotten luck, Cowans, Fowler and one I. T. Botham. My fingers were crossed for the three youngsters – more bad luck now could seriously damage their hopes for the rest of the tour – but I couldn't imagine anyone weeping tears for yours truly, not that I look for sympathy. Five years non-stop on the Test circuit have taught me to regard every tour as a single unit, a campaign to be won over a period of several months. There is no point in brooding over lack of success – much better to analyze your mistakes, seek out the advice of experienced people around you (oh, how we miss you, Ken Barrington!), and put them right by practice, practice and more practice. No touring cricketer these days needs to look far for the best possible advice when the press and commentary boxes hold such great past players as Fred Trueman, Tony Lewis, Trevor Bailey, Tom Graveney and Ted Dexter. And, if you ask them nicely, a few words of wisdom might be forthcoming from the Australian section – Richie Benaud, Keith Miller, Bill Lawry etc. – or even from Tony Greig of the League of Nations.

The match ended in a cliffhanger, with Bob Taylor and Bob Willis clinging on for a 1-wicket win. I managed to find some semblance of form with an innings of 65 and a 4 for 43 return in their second innings. The two Dereks, Randall and Pringle, got their heads down and soldiered well in a stand of 105, which turned the game our way. Also on the credit side was the vastly improved display of Norman Cowans. Bob Willis had been working hard with him in the nets, preaching the gospel of line and length, and he rewarded the skipper with a good fiery performance on a damp pitch to take 4 wickets in a spell of 25 balls, Graeme Wood, the Aussie opener, being among his victims. But there was still a good deal to worry about, too: Dennis Lillee and Terry Alderman took 16 of the 19 England wickets, Chris Tavaré bagged a pair, and Graeme Fowler was still a million miles away from the form he showed at Headingley on his Test baptism. Problems, problems, problems . . . and me a selector!

We had a few occasions for relaxation before the First Test, and in between net practices we made the most of them. Spirits were high, even though the time before the start of a series is generally a little anxious for some members of a touring party. Only wicketkeeper Ian Gould, a perky character with always plenty to say, and my Somerset buddy and off-spinner Vic Marks knew with certainty that they would be surplus to requirements in the First Test, but both were wise enough to know they had to stay sharp and match-fit, for their services were sure to be needed for the one-day tournament after the Test series. Both of them had had great success in one-day games at home. I was invited out, along with David Gower, Allan Lamb and Geoff Cook, on a private yacht. We were all grateful for the opportunity to sit back with a glass of Swan beer, free for a while from the pressures which seemed to be mounting daily. Several other players were taken out to see *Australia Two*, the local challenger for the 1983 America's Cup at Newport, Rhode Island. I gather they had a load of fun, with Derek Randall in his most irrepressible form. He gets more outrageous and unpredictable with the years, whether he's batting to save England at the crease or clowning about on the pride of Australia's yacht squadrons. It was soon clear to his hosts that this was no ordinary Englishman – for the *Australia Two* he promptly stripped down to his underpants and tied an 'Advance Australia' T-shirt around his head!

However we spent the time, the conversation was never far away from cricket, and the forthcoming Test. Most of the talk centred on the Perth wicket; both Bob Willis and the Western Australia captain, Kim Hughes, had criticized the track used for the match just finished. Bob said he thought it had favoured the bowlers too much; Hughes was more to the point: 'It was not really suitable for first-class cricket and is the worst I have seen here,' he said. I didn't think it was as bad as that, though deep cracks had appeared by the second day, causing the ball to deviate off line unexpectedly. It would be a different wicket for the Test; but even so my belief was that the wicket would probably favour the faster bowlers, in view of the good deal of movement and varying bounce it had offered in the State match.

It was most important that we should know exactly what kind of track curator John Maley had in store for us before we got down to selecting the side: when you've got five seamers and three off-spinners to choose from, a mistaken 'reading' of the pitch could be little short of disastrous. Maley is recognized as Australia's top groundsman, and he's also a very frank character. The trouble with the State wicket, he said, was that because of the unseasonably cool weather it had been given little chance to dry out. He uses just six wickets at Perth and believes the WACA wicket has seen its best days. Problems with acidity and salt build-up have increased the amount of dead roots in the wicket. Maley would dearly love to dig up the whole square, re-lay it, and get back to the fast wickets which charac-terized Perth Test matches of the past. I'm afraid Australian wickets have lost a lot of pace and there are now several in England which are quicker.

The state of the wicket, therefore, was high on the agenda when we selectors settled down in one of the hotel rooms for what looked like being a pretty long session. Right at the start, I said: 'It's vital that we don't lose the First Test. If we leave here one down, the rest of the tour will look like a mountain.' Bob was quick to follow with: 'Perth has always had a reputation for helping seam bowlers.' So the message was pretty clear: we would pack the side with four seam bowlers, and leave the spinning section to Geoff Miller, now that we had been assured he had recovered from a nasty crack on the right hand from a Lillee delivery in the last match. It was tough on Eddie Hemmings, who was proving himself a good tourist and had bowled successfully and intelligently in his two games so far. To be sure, his chance would come all too soon, but in the event the majority vote went to Pringle, possibly the better batsman and also a fourth seamer. Anybody reading this team as a 'holding operation' might not have been far off target. Avoidance of defeat was the prime consideration, as far as I was concerned.

Norman Cowans got the nod over Robin Jackman because, as Bob said, 'There's no point in holding him back.' As the question of openers was being discussed, I found myself thinking: 'If only Graham Gooch had turned down the lure of South Africa! I was beginning to feel concern for Graeme Fowler. So far his 8 innings had brought only 80 runs, and any hope he had had of gaining a Test place went with his dismissal by Dennis Lillee in both innings against Western Australia. Here was a young left-hander bursting with potential and always anxious to get the score rolling. Was it the extra pace, or bounce, or the light a few degrees brighter than at Old Trafford? Was it lack of confidence or simply lack of experience? Possibly a combination of all these factors, but he wouldn't be long in the wilderness, of that I was certain. 'Graeme is always full of beans,' I said, 'but as one failure has followed another, his mind must be in a bit of turmoil.' To expose him to the new-ball attack of Lillee and Alderman at this stage could have disastrous results – better to let him win back his confidence with the help and advice of those who have been around a bit longer. So Geoff Cook would partner Tavaré.

That evening, at the England team meeting and dinner, I took the opportunity to pass on two points of advice, both relating to Dennis the Menace. Point one was that in no circumstances should any of the players react if Lillee, as expected, started to play up, a well-known hometown tactic for Dennis: it had been in Perth in the First Test against Pakistan the previous summer that he had clashed with Javed Miandad. I pointed out that in these kind of incidents the batsmen quite often came off worse in terms of concentration. 'When Dennis starts his tricks, which are mostly pre-planned, we must put our heads down and ignore him,' and I looked at Derek Randall as I spoke. He had already had a small brush with Lillee during the game against Western Australia and knew well from experience what those 'tricks' are. They take the form of furious appeals, quite often totally unfounded, and followed by the ferocious glare at batsman and umpire, and a few muttered words aimed at anyone in earshot. I liked the description by Matthew Engel in the *Guardian*. 'Lillee had a number of furious appeals,' he wrote. 'He has now eclipsed all his rivals in this (Jackman has not had many opportunities on this tour), having evolved a style halfway between an eight-year-old's imitation of Tarzan and a Soviet prosecutor demanding the death penalty.'

My second piece of advice concerned the crowd, who could be counted on to give Lillee a lot of encouragement on his home ground.

'Don't let it affect you,' I warned, 'because if Lillee doesn't perform they could work against him.'

So back to my room halfway to the sky, a room instantly recognizable because it's always in such a mess. I must confess the place did look a shambles – cassette tapes of rock groups, some of them my favourite Dire Straits, littering the bedside tables and fighting for space with the clothes which, I should be ashamed to admit, were scattered over the chairs and floor. But at least I know where things are!

On the morning of the match to take off the tension a little I decided to do something about the growing pile of mail. On average I get anything from sixty to a hundred letters a week, mostly asking for autographs; if only people would send stamped envelopes it would save a lot of time and I might be a little better off. I get a great many letters from India and Pakistan, all extremely polite and, yes, often to Iron Bottom. One Indian 'regular' insists on addressing me as 'My Dear Great Bottom'. This particular morning I found a letter from an Australian who had a cricket museum in a country town and wanted me to provide him with a souvenir. I could supply him with Lillee's scalp, of course, but that might present a little difficulty. No doubt I'd think of something. Soon it was back to 6KY, with the announcer pausing to give Perth's weather for the day: 'Fine and dry with an early sea breeze . . . estimated temperature 82 degrees.' I crossed to the window to check the weather situation for myself. Ominously there was a lot of cloud cover which could make the day humid and sticky, perhaps dangerously so for the team batting first.

The clouds had cleared away when we got to the ground, and Greg Chappell was there striking the first blow by winning the toss under bright blue skies. Immediately the Australian Navy Police Band struck up with a celebratory tune. The toss at the start of the Test now forms part of the pre-match entertainment in Australia. There nobody has to speculate on the state of the wicket or wait for the captains to stroll back to the pavilion before hearing who had won. As soon as Greg Chappell had called correctly, his brother Ian thrust a microphone under his nose for the benefit of Kerry Packer's Channel Nine viewers and other cricket-lovers in all parts of the world.

'I'm not that concerned one way or the other. The Perth wicket will always have a bit for the bowlers early on,' Greg told Ian's mike, 'and I believe by putting England in to bat that our bowlers will have the best of the conditions, as will our batsmen later on in the match.' To judge from their public behaviour towards one another the brothers might just as well have been complete strangers. I remember a certain journalist telling me how Ian Chappell played hell on one occasion over a description of Greg as 'my brother Greg' in an interview written by a 'ghost'. Tough cookies, these Chappells!

The Freemantle Doctor, the south-westerly breeze which blows off the sea, was already stretching the Australian flag on the top of the nearby police headquarters when Tony Greig, the former England captain, walked to the middle for the now traditional pre-Test formalities. Greig, in his bright-blue Channel Nine blazer and MCC touring tie, peered at the wicket, explained for viewers what the tinge of green might mean for the bowlers, poked and prodded with his fingers and thumb, and then consulted a series of indicators to help him assess the day's weather. I reckon I could have told him there and then: Hot and sunny ... and aren't you lucky you're not playing, Tony! Now let's get on with the flippin' game.

Lillee opened, Cook faced. The first ball went swinging down the leg side and Australia's five slips and gully moved into conversation. The battle was on. We were soon struggling, as Cook went for 1 to Lillee after half an hour. I didn't think much of the Aussie openers: they wasted far too many balls, much of Lillee's bowling could safely be ignored, and when Geoff Lawson came on looking faster than anybody he also pitched too short. David Gower was batting as well as I have ever seen him, and Lillee was clearly rattled. Then he had an lbw appeal turned down and when Gower played his next ball gently down the pitch, Lillee kicked the ball angrily. Good old David remembered my briefing about Lillee, refused to be drawn and turned away as Lillee's words were volleyed down the pitch. Advantage, Gower!

Soon after this incident the crowd were banging the advertisement hoardings and chanting Lillee's name as he ran in to bowl, but nothing, it seemed, could disturb Tavaré's concentration. Eventually Gower left for a superb 72 (109 for 2) and Chris disappeared into his shell as Allan Lamb came, guns blazing. Again Lillee exploded when an appeal for a catch behind was turned down by umpire Tony Crafter. At the end of the over he snatched his sunhat angrily from Crafter and walked away, but this time Greg Chappell chased after him and presumably told him to 'cool it'.

At 4.45 on the first day Allan went to a catch behind off bat and pad so out I went to join the barnacle, the ever-patient Tavaré. I was pleasantly surprised by the reception the crowd gave me. Maybe they recognized me as a kindred spirit, a player who never pays much attention to outside influences. I like Aussies, I like their uncomplicated outlook on life and life's problems – but I'm not sure I like all their fast bowlers. That much-improved bowler Geoff Lawson was definitely gunning for me.

My innings lasted exactly one memorable over. First ball, nothing. Second ball, 2 off a full toss. Third ball, another 2 for, in fact, my 3,000th Test run. Fourth ball, slash over slips' heads for 4. Fifth ball, a smashing cover drive for 4 – even though I say it myself! Sixth ball, THE END – but what an end. I stretched forward as the ball cut back between bat and pad. I took my right hand off the bat in a high, arching movement and brought it down to indicate that the ball had brushed my pad. Rodney Marsh showed no great interest behind the stumps but Lawson's arm went up and instinctively he shouted for the catch, supported by a couple of Australian players. Umpire Crafter called the end of the over, handed Lawson his hat and then walked towards his fellow umpire Johnson, who had been standing at cover point to avoid the dipping sun. And then it happened. A minute after the original appeal Crafter raised his finger and I was given out, caught behind. I couldn't believe it possible. I thought I missed that ball by a good six inches. Can you wonder I swore to myself before tucking my bat under my arm and trudging back to the pavilion?

I accepted the decision without moaning because they have a different way of operating in Australia, and we have to play by their rules. Australian umpires make every decision. Sometimes you will win and on other occasions you will lose but you must be prepared to accept that under the Australian system. I swallowed my disappointment to watch Derek Randall, who seemed terribly nervous, but I was pleased to see he had taken my advice not to get involved in side issues with the Australian fast bowlers. He certainly seemed less fidgety than usual. Tavaré dried up completely, and didn't score a run in the last 70 minutes of the day, drawling to an unbeaten 66 in more than 6 hours. He came in for a lot of stick from the critics, particularly Keith Miller, a great name from the past, who thought his batting was about as exciting as watching paint dry. 'Boot him out,' wrote Miller, but I couldn't agree. True, Tavaré should have kept the score rolling in that last hour, as Bob Willis told him, but at the end of the day Chris told me: 'I have no special method for maintaining my concentration. I don't talk to myself or hum tunes. I think about nothing else but the job I am trying to do for England.'

Our methods may differ, I thought, but you'll do for me, Chris. And next day I marvelled once again at his dedication despite the crowd's constant barracking. Finally, when he was out for 89 after 466 minutes of superb concentration, we watched Derek Randall battle on to 78. He couldn't forgive himself for failing to make a ton. An hour after his dismissal he was still pacing around the dressing-room balcony. 'I missed, didn't I?' he moaned. 'I missed out. It was there . . . that's what it's all about.' But the real fireworks were just around the corner as the effects of the fierce sunshine and all-day drinking began to take its toll of one group of spectators.

Terry Alderman was bowling his 43rd over when England's captain edged the last ball of the over to the third-man boundary to bring up the 400. Alderman was tired and probably a little annoyed to see Willis get 4 runs for a false shot. From a spot immediately in front of a white caravan, which was being used for the sale of beer, a group of a dozen fans made their way on to the pitch carrying a Union Jack. Several were arm-in-arm, jubilant at England's performance and dismissive of Australian efforts to wrap up the innings. One young fan approached Alderman brandishing a small Union Jack and the West Australian fast bowler angrily pushed him away with both hands. As he did so another youth came up from behind and appeared to tap Alderman on the head, brushing his sunhat. Terry pursued his 'attacker' for twenty yards, bringing him to the ground with a rugby tackle. The crowd, at first stunned by what they were seeing, suddenly roared their encouragement. But Terry had fallen badly and injured his shoulder, through continuing to struggle with the fan until Lillee and Border ran to his assistance. Lillee held the youth in a headlock, but by now the fighting had spread to the terraces and for a few dangerous minutes the police could not control it.

Chappell took his team off the field, although Willis and the umpires wanted to stay on. Alderman had no choice – he was carried from the field on a stretcher by team-mates, his right arm held by our physiotherapist, Bernard Thomas. 'It is a very sad situation, but the cardinal rule is that players must not get involved with spectators,' Doug Insole told us. 'There is no mileage in taking them on.' The players were off the field for

14 concentration-shaking minutes, and when they returned Willis's defiance was quickly ended by Yardley, who also picked up the wicket of Cowans to finish with 5 for 107 in the England total of 411.

The fighting was a sickening and disgusting episode, as bad as anything I have seen on English television from the worst of our football 'supporters'. I believe alcohol was the main cause of this appalling demonstration, but there may have been another factor. Many true cricket-lovers are convinced that the television build-up to the series was badly conceived, and far from creating a healthy rivalry between the two opposing crowds, it achieved instead only a situation which required very little aggravation to produce a violence unknown in the long history of two friendly cricketing nations. The game cannot withstand such behaviour. It must be dealt with severely by the cricket authorities, by banning alcoholic drinks from all grounds if necessary, and by rigid vetting of all forms of advertising of forthcoming games. Whatever happens, this canker must not be allowed to infect our noble game. We have been warned!

The rest of the Test, I regret to say, came as an anti-climax and many of the players must have found it very hard to concentrate. Greg Chappell helped himself to yet another century, and I took an Australian wicket to set up a Test record of 250 wickets and 3,000 runs. The same I. T. B. also bowled 22 successive overs upwind, without a great deal of success, and Australia reached 424 for 9 before declaring. Bob Willis was disappointed with the bowling of Cowans and Pringle, and said so. 'Their overs should have cost fewer runs. They put too much pressure on Geoff Miller.' Geoff bowled very tidily and finished with 4 for 70 in 33 overs.

One wicket which gave me considerable pleasure was that of Rodney Marsh, whom I had caught swishing at a bouncer for a duck. At the end of the day I followed my usual habit of visiting the Australian dressing-room for a drink. The first person I looked for was Rod. 'Now, Bacchus,' I said, 'I want you to talk me through that shot. Take your time . . .'

The game eventually ended in a draw, though we came uncomfortably close to losing it at one stage. There were some hairy moments as our batting crumbled to 163 for 5 by the end of the fourth day – only 150 ahead and a whole day to survive! My contribution was nil, Geoff Lawson knocking my off stump back as I played hopelessly round the ball. 'I just didn't pick it up,' I explained later, 'and I can't account for it.' Later that evening, when I joined the Aussies for my usual drink, Rod Marsh came gunning for me. 'Now, Both,' he said, 'I want you to talk me through that innings. Take your time . . .'

Once again Derek Randall was our saviour. Resuming at 45 not out, he went out with Bob's orders for the day ringing in his ears: we must bat until the drinks period in between lunch and tea – some three hours at the crease. Derek took the hint and, though he lived dangerously at times, he survived. Time and again, fielders close to the bat heard him muttering to himself: 'Patience, patience! Don't do anything silly.' Bob Taylor helped him with a vital innings at the crucial stage – a good man for a crisis is old Bob – and Derek Pringle finally found his batting touch at the right time to give Randall further support. The Notts lad lunched nervously 3 short of his hundred, and when he resumed the battle against Lawson he played an over that is worth describing ball by ball, a vintage Randall exhibition.

Lawson's first ball was signalled wide and Randall kept the adrenalin going by jogging on the spot. The next ball again swung wide outside the off stump. Derek threw his bat into the air, caught it by the blade and trotted half-a-dozen yards towards square leg. The third ball from Lawson was short, again outside off stump, but again Randall wasn't interested. He swung his bat after the ball had passed him, thumped his pads and pulled at his left glove with his teeth. Lawson's next delivery went down the leg side and Randall's only reaction was to swat away a fly and kick the bowler's marks. 'Take your time, don't be rushed,' he chuntered to anybody within earshot, then went up and down on his toes as he waited for Lawson's fifth ball. It was short, rising outside the off stump, and this time Randall jumped, jabbed and missed as the ball went through to Marsh. He made contact with the next ball, sending it to Hughes at mid-wicket, but made no attempt to run. Lawson had a seventh ball to bowl, and for the last-day crowd of nearly six thousand the tension was electrifying. The bowler turned at the end of his run, Randall patted the crease and waited to receive the 197th delivery of his innings. The ball was on leg stump and Derek flicked it away to the fine leg boundary for his fifth Test hundred, his third against Australia.

Little Randall had done it again. He had come to the wicket at 4.25 the previous afternoon and by the time he was dismissed for 115 at 2.18 he had guided England to the safety of 292 for 8. When he chopped a ball from Lawson on to his pad and then on to the stumps, Derek simply bent down to pick up a bail, carefully replaced it and then tucked his bat under his

Jeff Thomson and Bruce Yardley congratulating each other on getting me out for 40 in the Second Test.

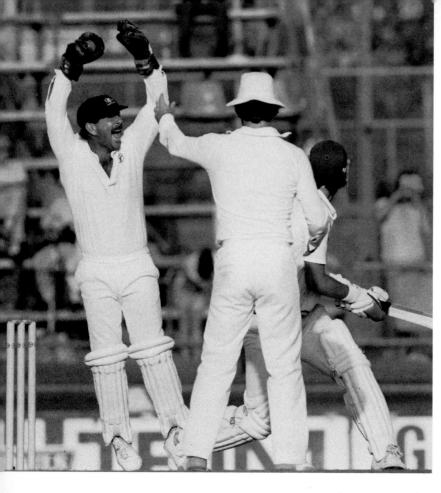

Below Rodney Marsh taking his 300th catch for Australia; *left* appealing for Geoff Miller's wicket, his 301st victim.

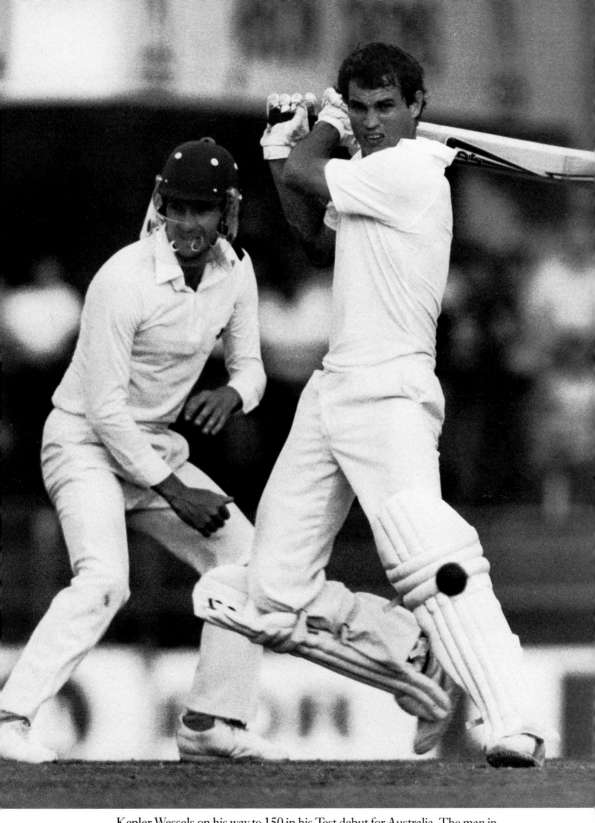

Kepler Wessels on his way to 150 in his Test debut for Australia. The man in the mask is Derek Randall.

Above: left Graeme Fowler on the receiving end of a bouncer from Jeff Thomson soon after the re-start of play in the Second Test; *right* Greg Chappell conferring with Umpire Bailhache over bad light this during Test. *Below* Yes, I missed a catch.

Kim Hughes hits out past David Gower to help Australia to a 7-wicket victory in the Second Test.

Left Greg Chappell escapes a bouncer from Bob Will
in the Third Test; *below* acknowledges the applause f
his century.

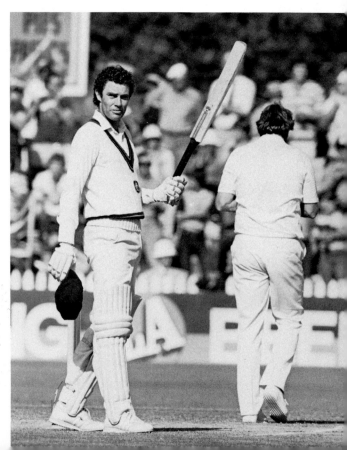

Allan Lamb in action in the Third Test;   Self; it wasn't all attack Down Under.

Jeff Thomson at full stretch during the Third Test.

arm for the slouching, tired walk back to the pavilion. Randall had denied Australia yet again and deservedly won the Man of the Match award. Willis allowed Pringle and Cowans to add 66 for the tenth wicket to make quite certain that England could not be caught. Then, in 95 minutes, Bob struck two important blows by removing Wood and Dyson cheaply, but Border and Chappell took Australia to 73 for 2 at the end of the match.

Afterwards our skipper showed concern for some of his players. 'There were some very good performances and some very moderate ones,' he said. 'Cowans is a very raw young man and he found the match a huge mental strain. But he is willing to learn and I'm sure he will be back. Botham can bowl a lot better and will do so before the series is out, while Tavaré is not really in great form. He must bat more positively.' Greg Chappell had no doubts about the reason for England's escape. 'Randall was the difference between a draw and an Australian victory,' he declared.

So we left Perth still on even terms, a position which we had been looking to achieve from the first morning when Australia won the toss. The game had been a delaying action by England but, as we headed for Sydney and the State match against New South Wales, the tour selectors were already thinking of making one major change for the second Test in Brisbane.

3

The Second Test, Brisbane

ON THE EVE of the Second Test in Brisbane, Dennis Lillee chose the Avro Room of the city's Park Royal hotel to attack the critics who were suggesting that his career as Australia's leading fast bowler was over. I could appreciate Dennis's anger. Next to being hit back over the head for 6, a fast bowler – even a thirty-three-year-old fast bowler – hates being told to go away and breed sheep.

Dennis, great fighter that he is, reacted predictably when people rushed to write him off after hearing of his operation in a Sydney hospital. After a general anaesthetic a tiny incision had been made in Lillee's right knee and a narrow instrument, an arthroscope, was inserted to probe the cartilage. A second instrument was then inserted inside the centre of the arthroscope and loose particles of bone were removed.

Lillee held up these bone flakes at the end of the press conference and joked: 'If these are being preserved in alcohol I had better put them away in case you blokes drink it.' Lillee's other comments reported in the following morning's newspapers were less flippant, as he sought to deny stories that his career would be cut short by the latest in a series of injuries. 'To be told that you are finished has bugged me a heap,' he said. 'I'm sick and tired of it. Why don't people believe me when I say I want to carry on?' I knew fellow-feeling for Dennis the Menace on that score. To be put on the defensive after being open in answering questions has the dual effect of sapping your efforts and making people believe rumours all the more.

Seven blocks across the city in King George Square, the England players also had Lillee on their minds at the pre-Test team meeting. Australia had brought back Jeff Thomson to partner Geoff Lawson, and when Lillee pulled out they sent for twenty-two-year-old Carl Racke-mann, the blond giant from the bush who had overcome a serious injury in his right shoulder. 'Australia will have three men who can bowl quickly in this game, but they don't move the ball around as much as Lillee,' said Willis, who predicted that the side winning the toss would probably put the other into bat.

Lawson had earned a lot of new respect after his performance in England's second innings at Perth; Rackemann, despite his period on the Surrey staff, was something of an unknown quantity after making an impressive start in the Sheffield Shield competition; and for those of us who had been blitzed by Thomson in the past, we knew just what to expect. Jeff's freaky action was talked about at the team meeting, and although we thought that maybe he had lost a bit of pace we expected him to produce something extra on his recall.

It had been at Brisbane that Thomson helped himself to 9 wickets against Mike Denness's team in 1974/5, including 6 for 46 in the second innings. For the benefit of those in the team who hadn't seen much of Thomson, I reminded them how disconcerting he could be – you never saw the ball until it reached the top of his delivery. He had returned from Australia's tour of Pakistan with a blistered foot and weighing a stone less than his best. 'He is still short of a gallop,' Greg Chappell told us, but in my book Thomson was a thoroughbred who would stay the pace. Not only that, but he, too, had started the summer as a 'back number' and you could feel his resentment at this, and the edge it gave his game.

Australia's other change from Perth brought in Kepler Wessels, the South African-born opener who had qualified to play for his adopted country and had now commanded a Test place after several fine perform-ances for Queensland. Wessels had settled in Brisbane after several years playing for Sussex and was running the Golden Goose newsagency in Adelaide Street when the Australian selectors decided that he should make headlines as well as sell them. We were not overjoyed to know that we would be up against him rather than the man he had replaced, West Australia's Graeme Wood. Wood always gives a bowler a bit of a chance and has been known to have the odd rush of blood to the head. Wessels, on the other hand, has remarkable concentration, even at Test level, where standards are enormously high.

We were forced to make one change because of injury ourselves when a ball I had let go during net practice the day before the match struck Geoff Cook in the ribs. The tour management must have thought I was becoming something of a liability – I had already put Ian Gould out of action after a training accident. Cook really could consider himself unlucky because he had shown signs of regaining his confidence in the State game against New South Wales, and had been given the vote in front of the out-of-form Fowler.

We had already decided to play Hemmings, and on the morning of the match it was decided that Cowans would be a better bet than Pringle on a wicket which looked as though it might have some pace early on. The theory was that Cowans had bowled well in the match against New South Wales: he had looked sharp, even fiery, at times. We thought that at Brisbane, where it can go through the top a bit, he would be an asset. When we lost the toss for the second time in the series – and were again invited to bat by Chappell – Willis walked back to the dressing-room with hopes that we ought to repond with a total approaching 400. We felt the Australian batting was suspect and Chappell's decision to put us in to bat was a clear indication that he felt the same way about ours. Both teams wanted the chance to go for an early kill. We desperately needed to find a reliable opening partnership: a tough job would be tougher if we were constantly up against fast bowlers buoyed by early success.

Forty minutes later, the captain was staring across the Gabba at a scoreboard which showed that England were 13 for 2 after losing both openers, Fowler and Tavaré, to Lawson. It was the last thing we wanted; with Lillee and Alderman missing from the Australian attack we had felt this was our chance to take the initiative and put their newcomers under pressure. Fowler had found himself thrust into the Test after 10 innings on tour had reaped him the unconvincing total of 106 runs. It was another big test for a young man who seemed to be carrying bad luck around in his cricket bag. Rackemann had been preferred to Thomson with the new ball, wrongly in my opinion, and Fowler took the opportunity to stroke another shot for 3 while the Queensland country boy was straining his considerable frame into the breeze.

A couple of runs off Lawson took Fowler to 7, but in Lawson's next over, he followed a ball angled wide of the off stump. He looked cramped for space and the control was missing as he stabbed towards gully where Yardley, the incredible Rubber Man, recoiled in mid-air to grasp a stunning right-hand catch. Twelve minutes later, at 11.40, Tavaré was also on his way as 8 for 1 became 13 for 2; a situation which was greeted with silent misgiving by the rest of the England players watching the action on closed circuit television in the sanctuary of the dressing-room.

Lawson, who had sat a university examination the previous day, clearly had England in his sights after his first Test successes at Perth. He was performing a lot better than we had anticipated: good stamina and better control. It wasn't sour grapes on my part, but I also thought that he was having more than his share of luck. Every time he hit an England player on the gloves, or found an edge, an Australian pair of hands seemed to be waiting to take the catch. Luck, though, is not a subject I like to dwell on for long. It is nearly always a case of swings and roundabouts, and on this morning it was our turn to be riding the not so merry-go-round.

Tavaré, fresh from his century which helped us to beat New South Wales, had managed just a single before he edged a knee-high chance to Hughes at third slip. Still, it might have been worse for us as Gower, on 1, glanced Lawson off the middle of the bat but straight into the hands of Thomson at leg slip. The chance was spilled – swings and roundabouts – although Gower seemed happy to continue playing the shot even with the Australians clearly attacking him around his leg stump. Thomson's miss was to start something of an epidemic of dropped catches which I blamed on the background at the tight Gabba pitch. There are several different backgrounds, in fact, and it is sometimes difficult for a fielder when the ball soars into the line of the greyhound track and then the crowd. A dozen or more chances were put down during the match, the majority of them by the Australians, but perhaps the most crucial by ourselves on the last day.

Lamb had arrived at the wicket just as two fast bowling changes were being made – Thomson for Lawson on the field and Lillee for Tony Greig in the Channel Nine commentary box. Thomson's first ball to Lamb was a bouncer. 'That's standard issue,' said Dennis. 'It's Thommo's way of saying "G'day, Sunshine".' Lamb must have thought that there wasn't much good about the day as Thomson threatened him with a number of short-pitched deliveries, but he survived the onslaught and had reached 33 not out when we lost the initiative in the over before lunch.

It might not have dawned fully on us at the time, but we were on the way to making a mess of things. Every time we got ourselves level on points, we dug a new hole to stumble into. Gower had batted 90 minutes and was on 18 when he attempted to steer Lawson away behind square leg. He played the shot a fraction late and Wessels leapt across from leg slip to pocket the catch at the second attempt. The skipper's indigestion at lunch wasn't caused by the food. 'It's self-destruction. Really, we must be more patient,' was his message, although, quite honestly, none of us needed telling.

The thought on my mind when I walked out to bat after lunch was that this was going to be a big innings, and for the first time in the series I got a really good start. Chappell surrounded me with three slips, two gulleys and a forward short leg, but the cordon behind the wicket wasn't enough when I cut Lawson above the heads of the gully fielders to the third-man fence. I was remembering the captain's words about patience, but knew that my best chance of succeeding was probably to play as naturally as possible.

I was getting the usual encouragement from the comedians in the crowd to 'Have a go, yer mug,' but this particular Pom wasn't going to be rushed. I had the feeling the fans half wanted me to fail, half wanted me to open up with some big hitting. During the early weeks of the tour, I frequently met this attitude from Australians wanting to buy me drinks as an excuse to talk about the Test series. I fancied the ordinary Aussie fan was praying for a home victory, but had a sneaking desire to see a touch of Botham belligerence as the Pommie ship went down. At this particular moment I was trying to stop our boat from rocking while remembering the lunch-time lecture from Willis.

Like Thomson, twenty-two-year-old Rackemann was perhaps straining a little too hard to achieve the next breakthrough and when he pitched short to me, I swatted him back over his head for 4. At the other end, Lamb had moved to his half-century by hooking Thomson into the fence for 4, but the next delivery was short again and this time Lamb swished unconvincingly, sending the ball in a slow loop to mid-wicket. Wessels, running from backward short leg, was only a yard short of reaching the ball before it hit the ground. We went through for a single and when Thomson's next ball was also an attempted bouncer, I took half a pace back, picked my spot, and cracked it over cover point to the boundary.

Thomson, maybe tiring of his short-pitched tactics, bowled the next delivery well up and I took the chance to hammer the ball back over his head for another 4. Jeff and I are old rivals and I felt we were both trying hard to come out on top in this early skirmish. Luckily, his line was a bit astray and when he next fired in a short ball outside leg stump, I swivelled into the shot and sent the ball over the fence and on to the greyhound track for 6. 'Pick the bones out of that, Thommo, old son,' I thought as he stared angrily down the wicket at me.

I fancied the wicket, I fancied the bowling and when the drinks interval arrived I thought that this could be the chance to launch our counter-attack. It was probably the first time on tour that I had begun by playing with so much freedom and as I sipped my drink and looked around the ground, I felt this was going to be my day. One banner being held up by the fans had caught my eye already. 'We're STILL waiting for Botham to tear us apart' it taunted – a reference to a television commercial in which a Smithfield meat porter was seen having a dig at the Aussies. The promotion of the Ashes series on television no doubt had a lot to do with the big crowds around Australia, but when the beer was flowing I couldn't help but feel that perhaps some of the commercials were a bit too stirring for the lads on the hill. By and large I thought the promotion of the Test matches and the one-day internationals was superb and surely it might now be time for Lord's to take a closer look at Kerry Packer's marketing techniques. The days are gone when you can simply stick up a poster outside a Test ground in England and expect the crowds to roll in. The Australian Cricket Board, through PBL Marketing, have found a wider audience for the game largely through the huge and mostly humorous television advertising.

My favourite television character was Nugget, a real Aussie bushman complete with corks on his hat who, in one particular commercial, came spluttering to the defence of Rodney Marsh after a Pommie voice had declared, 'He may not be the best wicketkeeper in the world, but he must be nearly the oldest!' Nugget shot back: ''Struth . . . did you hear that? He's talking about Marshie! Well, don't you worry, Rodney boy, there's more than one way to dong a wingeing Pom. You can hide their wallet under the soap . . . or whip the socks off 'em in cricket. And that's exactly what Australia's going to do to England in the big Benson and Hedges World Series Cup. Flaming hell, it's going to be the hottest cricket in a hundred summers . . . so don't you dare miss out.' A million spectators didn't miss out in Australia last summer, so I reckon Nugget must have done a pretty fair job for cricket.

The big crowds in Brisbane were hotting up nicely in the fierce sunshine as Yardley resumed the attack after the break and I responded by sweeping his third ball for 4. The next delivery was floated wide outside off stump and I stretched across to take the bait with an attempted square drive. My weight wasn't fully behind the shot and Rackemann, just behind point, gobbled up the head-high chance. No-one needed an honours degree in lip-reading to know exactly what I thought about the dismissal as I made my way angrily back to the pavilion. It had been a bad ball which deserved to be smashed for 4 and there I was looking up at the scoreboard and seeing that my innings was over for 40. Bad balls do get wickets, I should know that better than anyone; but the sick feeling in my stomach at that moment told me that I shouldn't have played the sucker on this particular occasion. I think I replayed the shot a hundred times in my mind that night and each time the ball crashed over the boundary for 4.

Before the match, Willis had talked about my lack of form on the tour at a crowded press briefing. 'Ian's frustrated and knows that he is capable of making a greater contribution. He's a pretty brave person, but the longer he doesn't succeed, the more this sort of thing is likely to get through to him.' I found it difficult to accept Bob's view that I needed to work harder at my game. I had never thought that things would be easy for me on the tour. Sometimes my attitude might appear carefree, but behind the bravado I fight as hard as the next bloke. It hurts to fail and, when I do, my optimism about the next innings should not be taken for a casual, couldn't-care-less approach. My dismissal by Yardley had come with the England total at 141 and only 11 more runs had been added when Lamb provided Marsh with his 300th catch in Test cricket.

Marsh had made his Test debut at the Gabba twelve years and eighty-eight Tests earlier, his first victim being Geoff Boycott, caught off the bowling of John Gleeson. Now, with Lamb swinging at a short ball from Lawson and mistiming the hook, Marsh threw himself to his left, taking his 300th catch high and left-handed. Later, Marsh played down this landmark. 'It meant nothing in itself,' he claimed. 'I was just happy that we had got rid of Botham and then Lamb, after they had been smashing us around the park for an hour.' Marsh will always have a place in my Test roll of honour. Once they called him old Iron Gloves, but his performances in recent years have made a mockery of that description. He has had his troubles with the Australian authorities, but most of his opponents will tell you that on the field he is a pretty fair competitor. The next ball brought Marsh his 301st victim when Miller got a brute of a delivery from Lawson. The ball arced off his glove and Marsh, running back, reached behind him to put us in all sorts of trouble at 152 for 6. I thought that Miller's batting had shown a lot of style in the early weeks of the tour and few players would have relished receiving a ball like that first up.

Lawson now had his tail in the air and although Taylor kept out his hat-trick ball he departed at 178, and any hope which we might have harboured of reaching a respectable total disappeared when Randall's sixty-six minute innings came to an end at 37. Willis fell quickly to Yardley and when bad light stopped play a few minutes before 5 pm Hemmings and Cowans had batted together for half an hour to take our first day total to 219, a situation which became 219 all out after just one ball from Lawson when play resumed on Saturday morning.

All ten of our wickets had fallen to catches, six of them resulting from attacking strokes. We had batted badly and we knew it. Four or five of us had got out by playing silly shots and after that it was all uphill. We cursed ourselves for letting the Aussies get their nose in front. Lawson, bowling a lot better than we thought he would, finished with 6 for 47 while Rackemann and Yardley picked up 2 wickets each. Thomson's 8 overs had cost him 43 runs without a wicket, but 'Two-Up' wasn't finished with this Test . . . not by a long way. Nor was Wessels who, for the next day and a half, more than confirmed our fears about his value to Australia. His strengths are the cut square of the wicket and the fullish drive on the offside. He picks up the majority of his runs in those areas and I was quite happy to feed him a few of his favourite shots early in the innings.

I'm a great believer in letting a batsman play in his quarter early on, because there is a great chance he will be lured into error by over-confidence. In Wessels's case, I gave him the opportunity to play his favourite cut shot but later switched to bowling straighter around middle and leg stump where he wasn't able to play with the same authority. Wessels's first runs in Test cricket were hooked forward of square leg off

Willis in the first over of the innings. Dyson got away with a single in my first over and then a push by Wessels brought Dyson back to face the final ball of the over. It was on a good length and Dyson played across the line, losing his middle stump as the ball found a gap between bat and pad. Australia were 4 for 1 and the members of the Queensland Cricketers Club were looking as raw as the underdone steaks sizzling on their pitch-side barbecue. When Border followed 7 runs later, caught by Randall at short leg, the members must have lost their appetites altogether.

We had planned to test Border with a couple of short-pitched deliveries early on, believing the Queensland left-hander would be apprehensive about his form at No. 3 in the Australian order. Personally, I thought Border was being sacrificed in that position and it was no surprise when Chappell promoted himself to No. 3 in the next Test at Adelaide. The delivery from Willis climbed into Border's body and, when he instinctively thrust his bat at the ball, it popped up for Randall to take the catch. The England captain's response was to pump his fists into the air, a show of excitement which became increasingly rare as the match progressed. Border dejectedly made his way back to the dressing-room, crushed by his failure. 'That's the way it goes when things are running against you,' he muttered. 'The ball could have fallen clear, but instead went straight to a fielder.' I was glad to see the back of Border but nevertheless I couldn't help but feel a touch of sympathy; it's always sad to see a fine player struggling – even when he is playing for the other side. Most of us felt Border would produce a big score before the series was over but were grateful that this wasn't going to be the day when he did it.

Chappell didn't take long to size up the situation when his arrival at the crease again prompted us to test him with several short-pitched deliveries. The Australian captain, noticing that there was no third man, helped himself to a couple of boundaries by lifting Willis over the heads of the gully fielders. At the other end, Wessels was in no mood to hurry after waiting four years to qualify for Australia. You could sense his determination as he moved to 50 with 3 runs through extra cover off Willis. Wessels immediately blessed himself, an act he later repeated when he reached his century. 'I was a member of the Dutch Reformed Church in South Africa and have always been a practising Christian,' he explained in a newspaper interview. 'My cricketing ability is a gift from God. It is up to me to make the most of my talent and I am always grateful when I succeed. Playing for Australia means everything for me now. I'm here to stay for keeps.'

Unfortunately for Wessels and Australia, Chappell wasn't there for keeps after taking 53 runs off 67 deliveries and looking capable of tearing us apart. He played a ball from Hemmings to cover and took off for a run which Wessels wisely decided wasn't there. Chappell took longer to reach the same conclusion and when he turned to regain his ground, Miller's throw was already on its way into Taylor's gloves. Chappell and Wessels had added 83 runs in 89 minutes with the Australian captain again singling out Cowans for special treatment. The young Middlesex bowler conceded 24 runs in his 5 overs and was then banished to the outfield by Willis for the best part of a day's cricket. 'There is no way you can gain experience standing around in the field,' said a critical Lillee in the commentary box.

Willis's view was that Cowans was between two stools: he wanted to bowl fast while still trying for line and length. The result was a succession of half volleys and long hops. The captain wanted him to concentrate on bowling flat out 'because that's what he has come out here for'. Willis had been impressed by the bowling of Cowans against New South Wales, but now, with the pressure on, he reasoned that he couldn't afford to take a gamble with a raw player. It was a delicate decision to make because Bob had to gamble that big Norman's temperament would stand up to treatment which, on the face of it, looked harsh. Cowans was given plenty of time to think about his approach while patrolling the boundary for over after over, and I don't think there was anyone in the team who didn't feel some sympathy for him. But this was Test cricket, after all, and no-one should need a nursemaid at this level.

Chappell had departed at 94 and 5 runs later we climbed back into the game when Hughes touched my big outswinger into the gloves of Taylor. Hookes began menacingly with 4 boundaries, but then Miller turned the ball past his forward defensive shot, also into the hands of Taylor. A couple of half-hearted appeals were enough to give umpire Robin Bailhache the chance to raise his finger, but no-one watching on television or studying the replays afterwards reckoned that Hookes had come within three inches of touching the ball. Once more, though, we were simply letting the umpires make the decisions without question. Right or wrong.

Marsh batted very much out of character for 42 minutes before he became the sixth Australian wicket to fall. He attempted to cut, found himself cramped for space, and snicked a catch to Taylor. Australia were 171 for 6, a position from which we believed we could win the match if we could get all our big guns to fire together. But Wessels, now joined by Yardley, would not be moved as he spent 45 minutes in the nineties, unperturbed and seemingly oblivious of the fact that he was about to become the thirteenth Australian to hit a century in his maiden Test match. At one point a woman in the crowd screamed, but it wasn't wife Sally, watching her husband's epic effort from the shade of the stands. Willis must have felt like screaming himself as he walked tiredly back to the end of his run, blowing hard and then gritting his teeth as he turned to steam in for his seventeenth over of the innings.

Wessels cut to Cowans at third man and jogged through for the single. Ninety-five and the crowd were baying for more. Willis removed himself from the firing line and Wessels removed his helmet before sweeping Hemmings for another run. Ninety-six and the tension was being heightened by Yardley's exaggerated efforts at concentration at the other end. Several times Yardley connected and several times he missed, stamping away from the crease in annoyance. We weren't much amused either because Yardley didn't figure too highly in our shortlist of batsmen to fear.

Wessels was like ice at the other end, taking a single off Miller to mid-wicket. Ninety-seven. Nothing, it seemed, could disturb him, not even when Hemmings beat the bat on the forward defensive and Taylor missed a difficult stumping chance. Wessels was prepared to wait for the right ball after batting for most of the day and when Hemmings, in the next over, pitched short on leg stump, Wessels gratefully pulled it away to the boundary for his hundred. He made the sign of the cross and then thrust out his right hand to accept the congratulations of first Yardley and then Willis. He deserved his moment of glory. It had been a good innings, motivated, I'm sure, by the fact that he was playing his first Test for his new country.

Australia had begun the third day at 246 for 6 and although Willis had already made it known that we had lost our chance of victory with poor batting on the first day, our performance on the field that morning, a Sunday, clearly upset him. There was cloud and the odd spot of rain. A stiff breeze tugged at the numerous flags around the ground as Willis took the new ball for the first over of the day. At the other end, I began by conceding 7 runs in my first over, 4 of them flying off Yardley's bat over the head of Fowler at deep point. Here we go again, I thought, and, sure enough, another Yardley slash took the ball over the heads of the slips cordon and into the fence for 4. We thought we had just about sorted out Yardley by using a couple of fly slips at Perth, but here he was finding the gaps and driving us to frustration. Willis looked annoyed; he didn't need to say anything for the rest of us to know he didn't consider we were doing our jobs.

Any displeasure, though, never reached the point, as some critics tried to suggest, that Bob and I had stopped talking because of a rift between us. It's easy to misinterpret things from a hundred yards away. The previous day, for instance, the skipper had moved me to silly point for Wessels. I didn't think it was a good idea and after one ball I asked Bob who he would have to bowl if I were rapped on the shins. He saw the sense of that and immediately switched me into the covers. Hardly the start of a rift which allegedly built up into a breakdown of communication. I've never been afraid to speak up if I feel I have something useful to say, but in the end I will always back the captain right along the line.

Yardley reached his fifty with another flailing cover drive off my bowling, but in Willis's next over he edged a chest-high chance which was taken by Tavaré at second slip. Yardley and Wessels had added 100 together and the game had been turned back Australia's way at 271 for 7. It was a bad morning session for me; I hadn't bowled as badly for two years and Wessels took full advantage. Willis was in a dilemma which he tried to sort out by bringing Cowans on for only his sixth over of the innings. It was 11.35 and he had not bowled since the first session the previous morning. Cowans's second ball was overpitched outside off stump and Wessels guided it to the third man fence for 4. His fifth ball was a half volley and Wessels stretched on to the front foot and crashed it through extra cover to the fence.

Willis signalled Tavaré to move from second slip into the covers, but Wessels found another gap off the final ball of the over, this time backward of point for his third boundary of the over. Willis strode angrily from his position at mid-off without a word to Cowans, who found himself back in the outfield for the rest of the innings. Bob seemed reluctant to talk to anyone in the team as he set about finishing off the Australian innings almost single-handed. He was in one of his super-charged moods when he won't hear of failure. I didn't help by dropping Lawson at third slip but fortunately the same player swung Willis into the hands of Hemmings at backward square leg. Willis then bowled Rackemann before ending the defiance of Wessels, who went for 162 in Australia's total of 341, a first innings lead of 122.

Willis, who finished with 5 wickets, took his sweater and walked off alone, remembering to pause at the gate and applaud Wessels into the pavilion. I don't think many of the rest of us felt we deserved any applause for our efforts that morning. It had been a sloppy performance in some respects, leaving us with a feeling that we had forfeited the chance of pulling Australia back to level terms.

The Australians gave us a chance by spilling several catches at the start of our second innings. Tavaré was dropped by Dyson off Rackemann and Fowler had a change of luck at 21 when he edged Rackemann into the slips cordon where Hughes fumbled the chest-high chance before pushing it in the direction of Hookes, who juggled and finally dropped the ball. It was like something out of a Marx Brothers comedy, only few in the England dressing-room could appreciate the funny side of it. Two runs later Fowler began to walk, believing he had been caught by Wessels at short leg, but umpire Mel Johnson had his arm raised for a no-ball by Rackemann. Australia's only success before stumps came when Tavaré glanced Lawson to Marsh with the score at 54, leaving Fowler and Gower to negotiate a tricky final period when the players returned to the field after a lengthy break for bad light.

Gower was clearly unhappy with the conditions and annoyed Chappell by prodding the wicket and peering at the sightscreen in a move aimed at wasting time. 'The light's okay, get on with it,' snapped Chappell. Gower gave him a very frosty look but said nothing. Thomson, whose bowling had been strained in the first innings, was suddenly basking in a situation in which the batsmen found the odds mounting against them. This was just like old times for Jeff and in his excitement he kept firing the ball in short.

The bouncer which broke umpire Bailhache's patience was the one which fizzed around Fowler's ears soon after the re-start. Thomson, who had been warned already by Bailhache for intimidatory bowling, was forced to leave the field again when the officials decided that the light had suddenly deteriorated. Only Chappell stayed behind to argue publicly his case over what was considered by the umpires to be intimidatory bowling. 'Please,' said Chappell to the umpires, 'what are your guidelines for short-pitched bowling? It helps everybody if the system is clarified.' Bailhache walked off without a smile and a few days later announced his retirement from Test cricket.

On the rest day Willis spoke of his two biggest problems in the fight to save the match. He thought I was still frustrated by my lack of form and could find room for improvement by putting more into my preparation. I didn't think I could do any more but a relaxing day spent at the home of Allan Border and his family gave me the opportunity to think about my approach. It was something of a no-win situation. My instincts told me to keep playing my natural game and ignore the outside pressures which were building up. Aggression has always been the major part of my game and I didn't feel I would be serving the team best by becoming too conscious of the need for restraint.

The skipper's other cause for concern was Cowans, who thought that he had let everybody down with his bowling in the first innings. He couldn't find the right approach. He wanted the new ball but realized he wasn't bowling well enough to command it. He needed wickets but without the new ball how was he going to get them? He thought Greg Chappell had adopted a deliberate policy of trying to hit him out of the firing line, knowing that his own place in the Australian team was not in danger if he failed. Cowans felt the difference in being brought on when the batsmen and not the bowlers were on top. Some of us thought that maybe he lacked a little bit of devil in his bowling, though probably this part of his game might improve when he regained confidence.

Australia began the fourth day's play without Rackemann, who had suffered a groin injury, and they proceeded to make life even more difficult for themselves by dropping several catches. Gower, on 5, was dropped off Thomson by Hughes at third slip. Then, amazingly, Marsh put down Fowler when he flashed wildly in Thomson's next over. Fowler reached his fifty with an outside edge over second slip but looked a little embarrassed to acknowledge the crowd's polite applause.

Just before lunch we were 144 for 1 and very close to saving the match. At tea, we were 206 for 6 and very close to losing it. What went on in between largely revolved around Thomson, who came pounding in with all the old, coiled menace of past seasons to take 5 wickets for 12 runs in 8 overs. He started by removing Gower, who the previous evening had sat in a Brisbane fish restaurant and talked about the looping bounce of the Gabba wicket. Some of the short-pitched deliveries, he argued, didn't come through as fast as expected. Gower's dismissal after batting for two hours and fifteen minutes illustrated that point: Thomson pitched short on leg stump, the ball appeared to hang in the air and Gower was through his shot a fraction early. It touched his glove and Marsh did the rest behind the wicket.

Lamb had opened confidently with a couple of boundaries before lunch but a refreshed Thomson hurried him into a false stroke soon after the resumption and we were rocking in the breeze at 165 for 3. I had been suffering from a migraine attack over lunch and it was decided to send Randall in ahead of me, but he became Thomson's next victim at 169 after a stunning catch by Yardley in the gully. I was aware when I walked out that England needed a big innings from me and I tried to relax mentally as I watched Chappell set his field. He put two men on the fence on the on-side for the hook and a third man ten yards from the fence for the lofted cut, but I contented myself with a couple of singles before Lawson came on to give Thomson a breather. Thomson went to deep backward point and that was where my full-blooded but lofted shot, found him. The catch came at knee height, in and then out of Thomson's hands. I was furious at walking into Chappell's trap. How could I have been so damned stupid?

Fowler, on 83, was next to go, guiding a Thomson bouncer outside leg stump into the gloves of Marsh. It hadn't been a classic innings, as Fowler was quick to acknowledge, but it had had courage and tenacity, qualities which we were in the mood to appreciate. I was still curbing my natural game and perhaps showing too much inhibition when I went to hit Thomson, changed my mind and finished up cramped for space and edging a catch to Marsh. The delight of the Australian players only added to my disgust.

The later defiance of Miller, who ended the day with an unbeaten half-century, and that of Hemmings, sticking fast for 18, gave the faintest hope of a dramatic finish but Willis was among those who believed that our chance had gone once our final 3 wickets produced only 30 more runs on the final morning. Lawson claimed all 3 wickets to finish with 5 for 87 alongside Thomson's 5 for 73 in our second innings total of 309, which left Australia to bat again at noon, needing 188 runs for victory.

There were five hours remaining in the Test; I could imagine there might be just a touch of apprehension in the Australian dressing-room. We were thinking about Headingley the previous summer, but it was no more than a half hope at the back of our minds. Yet another 50 and we'd be in with a chance. We needed to strike a couple of decisive blows early in the innings to put the Australians under pressure, but one chance went begging in the first over when Wessels drove at Willis and Fowler dropped a pretty straightforward catch at cover. I think the Australians would have won even if Fowler had held on to the chance, but psychologically it was a bad miss.

Dyson was forced to retire with a badly bruised shoulder after being hit by Willis and with the wickets of Border, Chappell and then Wessels falling for 83, we were hanging on by our bootlaces. Even when I returned for my third spell, I thought that we were not quite out of it, but when Hookes missed an attempted pull off a ball which kept low and hit him on the pads, umpire Bailhache turned down my appeal and our last chance was gone. Hookes was still there at the end with Hughes to steer Australia to a 7-wicket victory which they deserved for their more consistent bowling. We'd been outgunned, not because our firepower was any less than Australia's but because we'd fumbled on the draw.

One of the few things to give us a lift that afternoon was a first Test wicket for Cowans – Greg Chappell at that. Cowans had been brought on for the second over after lunch, and from the final ball Wessels edged between Miller at first slip and Tavaré at second. Cowans stood there with his hands on his hips looking like the world had fallen in on him. Consolation came in the next over when Chappell hooked him for the second time in his innings, but this time Lamb was waiting under the ball and took the catch comfortably at deep backward square leg. For a couple of overs Cowans bowled with the fire we had hoped he might produce when he came to Australia. The wicket of Chappell had given him a lift but still the effort couldn't tilt the game back our way. Several times in this Test we had threatened to get our noses in front, but on too many occasions we had heedlessly tossed the advantage away. The skipper was calling for patience in our batting, but after losing in Brisbane I believed we also needed a more positive attitude when we moved on to Adelaide. I had the feeling that something was missing from our approach, but at that moment I had difficulty putting my finger on the problem.

4

The Third Test, Adelaide

I APPRECIATE FAILURE about as much as a Dennis Lillee bouncer between the eyes. It hurts my pride and churns my stomach. I don't think I will ever come to terms with being beaten, whether it's by my wife Kathy on the tennis court or by Australia in a Test match. Our defeat at Brisbane had been painful enough but I was sure it would not prove fatal. We had to come back hard. We had to get it right and that included making the correct decision if we won the toss for the first time in the series. With that in mind, a group of us stood in the centre of the Adelaide Oval discussing the wicket twenty-four hours before a ball was due to be bowled. The England captain, manager and senior players, including myself, peered at a strip, prepared by groundsman Les Burdett, which contained enough moisture to allow a thumb to be pressed into the surface on a good length. A day later our little group of supposedly wise heads and lion hearts was back in the middle looking at a wicket which had dried out sufficiently to give every indication that it would be firm and flat.

I was aware that only three captains had gambled on sending the opposing team in to bat in the previous twenty-two Australia-England Tests at Adelaide Oval – and each of them had been soundly spanked as a result. To hell with it, I thought. My own experience of Adelaide suggested that any life in the wicket would be in the opening session and as we were behind in the series I reckoned we must attack. What was the point of pussy-footing around, I argued; if we didn't get into Australia's ribs from the start we might never get another chance.

When Willis won the toss and chose to put Australia in to bat, the criticism came tumbling down on his head like an earthquake at Ayers Rock. The locals believed he had misread the pitch. He was accused in one of the Adelaide papers of playing Father Christmas to Australia's cricketers; when I read that my blood boiled. The truth of what happened out in the middle on the morning of the Test was that the skipper was inclined to bat first if he won the toss. He listened to everybody else's opinion and was persuaded to take the opposite line. I was among those who had argued in favour of bowling first, and although the ultimate decision is the captain's I naturally felt sympathy for him. It was all very well for people to be smug after the event, but I knew that Greg Chappell had planned to ask us to bat had he been given the chance. I could quite imagine Chappell's relief when he saw the expected early life in the wicket didn't materialize.

The middle-aged ladies in their summery hats were comfortably seated in the shade of the members' stand and the bikini-clad girls on the hill were attracting their first wolf whistles when Willis ran in to bowl the opening delivery of the Test to Dyson on the stroke of eleven o'clock. We were all anxious to discover signs of life in the wicket, no-one more so than the skipper; but it didn't look good. When I pitched short to Wessels he had too much time to pull the ball in front of square for 4. No-one said anything, but it didn't take long for most of us to make up our minds that we would rather be batting than bowling. So much for my reputation as a reader of wickets.

I had gone into the Test with a niggling pain in my back. It wasn't the old trouble which had hampered me a couple of summers previously, but it was persistent enough to defy the healing hands of physio Bernie Thomas. I tried to force the thought of injury out of my mind, but while I was reasonably successful at fooling myself I couldn't pull the wool over the eyes of an old pro like Dennis Lillee. It didn't take him long to write in one of his newspaper columns that I looked to be in pain. Dennis should have known that fast bowlers don't fade away without a fight and I reckoned I was best serving England by being out in the middle and not propped up on a pillow in the dressing-room. In any case, I'm an awful spectator; even when I'm actually playing in a game I can only half watch the action. It's a form of superstition, really. I play cards, doze or sign autographs – anything, in fact, to avoid watching the cricket which, it seems to me, brings bad luck to the batsman.

We had been looking for at least three wickets in that first session of play on the opening morning; Dyson came close to providing us with the first when he gloved one off me and it looped over the head of Eddie Hemmings at backward short leg. Eddie might not be the fleetest mover in the team, but I think even England goalkeeper Peter Shilton might have struggled to get a hand on the ball as it lobbed tantalizingly. I wasn't totally satisfied with my first spell and asked Willis if I could follow him at the River End, bowling with the help of a stiffish breeze. He agreed, replacing me with Pringle, who had bowled pretty well in the State game against Victoria in Melbourne, taking four wickets; next to Geoff Miller, he was the pick of the bowlers. Miller had long spells in each innings, bowling economically to collect 6 wickets in the match. Norman Cowans wasn't completely fit and we reasoned that the Adelaide wicket wouldn't have too much pace for him. Our batting heroes in Melbourne were David Gower and Allan Lamb with a second innings century. I failed in both Victoria innings, managed only a couple of wickets and left a drawn match hoping that my form would improve at Adelaide. Now, with Willis needing a breather, here was my chance. I'd been content to pace myself in the State games, saving my energies for the Tests; I was aware that unless I performed in the big matches I would lay myself open to strong criticism. I admit I'm not the world's most dedicated trainer; but then I never have been and no-one has ever had cause to question my stamina, even when I've kept my fifteen and a half stone on the move in the heat for half a day. In fact I've seen plenty of younger fast bowlers flagging after doing only half as much; so carping about my fitness is guaranteed to get me as angry as an Aussie in a pub with no beer.

Willis bowled 8 overs before coming off with the Australian total showing an ominous 47 without loss. But a little bit of luck was around the corner when I misdirected a delivery to Wessels, firing it outside his leg stump and giving him the opportunity to glance it into the hands of Bob Taylor. I had bowled many better balls that morning, so I had to have a little chuckle to myself when Kepler presented me with his wicket that way. Still, luck always evens itself out in the end and I made a mental note to be gracious next time Wessels snicked me over the heads of the slips. So much for good intentions – when Dyson later slashed me into Gower's hands at gully and the chance went down, I didn't stand there mildly ruminating on the bitter-sweet life of a Test fast bowler: I was furious. Luckily, and much to Gower's relief, Dyson went 1 run later when he fended at a ball which I got to leave him off the wicket. Taylor did the rest to leave Australia at 138 for 2, a fair enough position which looked even better once Chappell went in search of his first ever Test century at the Adelaide Oval.

Chappell had been in tremendous form right from the start of his innings and, typically, he stepped up a gear once he felt he was being challenged. A Willis bouncer which knocked Chappell off balance and sent him squirming into the dust lit the touchpaper on a furious assault. The next ball from Bob was steered behind point for 4 and then a thunderous cover drive underlined the message from the Australian skipper. 'Don't mess about with me,' seemed to be the general drift. I could only stand back and applaud when he crashed me off the back foot to the extra cover boundary for his fifty; from that moment until he was dismissed 11 minutes before stumps, one felt inevitably that Chappell was heading for a momentous century, that he wanted to do something special on the ground where his uncle, Victor Richardson, had performed so magnificently for Australia. He seemed to have got it into his mind in this series that the best way of countering us was to attack, a tactic which he followed through to perfection in this Test. There was an arrogance about Chappell's approach which I felt he was injecting into the rest of his team, something I've seen before, notably in the West Indies; and I began to worry that the Australians were edging ahead of us in self-belief.

At one point in the afternoon I thought we would be looking at an Australian total of around 600 but, with a little bit of advice from Bob Taylor, we managed to slow down the Adelaide express. Bob suggested that he stood up to Kim Hughes, who likes to get his front leg down the wicket: there was a chance he might get himself in the wrong position and offer a stumping opportunity. The ball was about 50 overs old; on that track it was hardly bouncing and seaming around, so I was quite happy to go along with the ploy. We had to do something to pull them back and my method was to settle for line and length; when I studied the figures afterwards I believed it was the correct decision. My first 10 overs had cost me a fair few runs, but in the rest of the innings I managed to keep a tighter rein, even though the Australians were on the attack. Eddie Hemmings also did a good job for us, toiling away for long periods without an awful lot of luck. Eddie looks to spin the ball more than either Geoff Miller or Vic Marks and in a defensive situation he kept the lid on the Australian innings.

Our biggest slice of luck came on the second morning when Hughes and Border were involved in a real mess-up just as they were threatening to torture us in the near hundred-degree temperature. Hughes had played a controlled knock and given us little encouragement for a change . . . we usually feel that even if he gets to 30 there's a fair chance he will throw it away. This time Hughes got to 88 before he and Border hesitated disastrously – and the Australian vice-captain was left stranded in mid-wicket. So, though we weren't exactly doing handstands round the dressing-room after Australia had been bowled out for 438, the feeling was that it could have been a lot worse. We had egg on our face, but it could so easily have been the bacon and frying pan as well.

I think most of us were of the opinion that on a reasonable wicket like this one we should survive, and not even Tavaré's dismissal for 1 and Fowler's exit for 11 could alter that feeling. Chappell had given Rodney Hogg the new ball with Lawson and he responded with a lightning 6-over spell before stumps. Hogg has always been the pick of the Australian fast bowlers as far as I am concerned and it is ironic to think that but for the injuries to Alderman, Lillee and Rackemann he might have been squeezed out of the series. But with the ball once in his hand there seemed no way he was going to give the selectors the chance to snatch it back. Hogg's only problem is his stamina and when we woke up on Sunday morning to a beautiful blue sky which was quickly shimmering in the heat we all believed that this was our chance to make the Australian fast bowlers suffer. And that opinion hadn't changed at lunch when Gower and Lamb had taken the score to 140 for 2 and we were giving every appearance of piling on the runs in the afternoon.

What happened in the next session was a collapse for which there seemed no easy explanation. The bowling wasn't that good and the batting wasn't that bad, but somehow we contrived to lose 8 wickets cheaply and found ourselves following on around teatime. I stood at the other end and watched 3 of those wickets fall, including that of Lamb in controversial circumstances. He tried to swing Lawson behind square and when Marsh jubilantly raised his glove in the air, umpire Mel Johnson upheld the appeal. I reckoned Lamb hadn't hit it; so did he, but yet again the Aussies had proved the value of giving it a big shout when they made an appeal. All through the series I was concerned that we didn't really give it all we had when we appealed. The Australians believe the umpire is there to make

decisions and you don't make them for him. If you think you have a
chance of getting away with it, you stay in your ground and don't 'walk'.
It's all very well for people to say that's not playing the game but this
is our living, after all, and I believe it should be a case of 'When in
Rome . . .'

Randall and Miller were the other batsmen to go while I watched with
my heart sinking at the other end. Randall was unlucky when the ball came
back off his pads and on to the stumps. I think it would have missed by six
inches, but I fancy he didn't pick up the ball too well from Lawson. Here
we go again, I thought. Five down for 180-odd and when Bob Taylor
didn't hang around long enough to get a sweat on his shirt, the follow-on
figure of 239 suddenly looked a menacing target.

I had to decide in my own mind the right form of attack. I had been
feeling in pretty good nick, especially after crashing Lawson off the front
foot for 4 through cover, and then repeating the treatment in Yardley's
next over. I could have gone into a shell, hoping to chisel a few runs while
the others hung on at the other end, but that's not really my style and in
this situation I didn't feel it would be in the interests of my side. Our tail
hadn't been too effective so far in the series and there was no guarantee
that they would be any more prolific against a keyed-up Australian attack.
Pringle was clearly finding the step up to Test cricket a tough experience.
Lawson, Hogg and Thomson in full flight were a much more formidable
test than facing second-string attacks on a flat wicket at Fenners. Derek
likes to get on to the front foot, hitting the ball in the arc between extra
cover and mid-wicket, but against consistently short-pitched bowling on
Australian wickets his opportunities were rare. Like Fowler, though, one
felt he was slowly coming to terms with the job and would be a better
player for the experience.

For the moment, though, I felt I should try to take charge and
attempted to keep the strike by looking to hit fours and twos. I needed to
find the gaps and against an attack which by now must have been feeling
the heat, I moved along to 35 sweetly enough. Then Thomson over-
pitched on leg stump, I aimed to work the ball away through mid-wicket
and watched in horror as it lofted into the hands of Wessels. The innings
lasted only 10 more balls and we found ourselves trailing, quite unbeliev-
ably, by 222 runs on the first innings. It was one of the low points of the tour
and when Tavaré departed for 0 when we batted again, we were well and

truly in trouble, even though Fowler and Gower got their heads down and batted bravely to take us to 90 for 1 at the close.

We had screwed up the follow-on and then lost an early wicket, but the mood in the dressing-room was far from despair. We were encouraging each other with the thought that if we could get 400 in the second innings, the Aussies would be denied the time to force a victory. We believed that a draw for us would have the psychological effect of a defeat on Australia and from there we would be in a position to hold on to the Ashes. We had the rest day to relax our bodies and direct our minds to what I believed would be perhaps the most crucial day of the series so far.

I took the opportunity to fly off with Greg Chappell and Rodney Marsh in a helicopter to the winery at Yalumba, a trip that has become a tradition for the players on the rest day in Adelaide – everyone should have a relaxing time, eating good food and drinking fine wines in between dips in the swimming pool or breathless backhands on the tennis court. I thoroughly enjoyed myself over a drink with Dennis Lillee, but unfortunately made the mistake of thinking that this was a private day. Perhaps I should have kept my shirt on – or stayed in bed all day – because it didn't take long for the photographers to start snapping once I had put my bathing trunks on for a swim. Some people seem to be obsessed by my weight and while I'll admit I'm no seven-stone weakling, I can't help but think that they only start talking about my belly when my batting or my bowling is not grinding rivals into the dust. I like a good meal and I'd be lying if I denied that I didn't enjoy a cold beer in good company at the end of a hard day's play; but that has always been my approach and it has never affected my performance on the field. The newspapers want me to be a larger-than-life character when I am doing well, but as soon as my form drops a fraction, those qualities are used against me. I don't seem to remember the likes of Colin Milburn and Colin Cowdrey getting the same degree of criticism when they were performing for England. The Australians have an expression 'Life, be in it' and I reckon that's a pretty good philosophy. I haven't yet decided what I'll do when I pack up cricket, but if a white-bearded I. T. Botham survives to tap his way around with a walking stick, I don't want him to feel he's missed out in any way.

The short break at Yalumba was a chance to take stock as well as to rest, and to think about our own and the public's reactions to the cricket being played. It wasn't easy for the England side to arrive in Australia dubbed, unfairly, in my view, a bunch of no-hopers who would have been better off staying at home stoking the winter fires. Since the series I've looked through other England teams that had been built up as something special and can only think that time fogs the memory in a big way. Sure, there were great players in those teams, but look beyond the star names and there were some pretty ordinary performers at Test level. Now, I don't know how the 1982/3 England touring team will be regarded in years to come, but I doubt if its reputation will be anywhere near as bad as some people tried to make out after our early struggles. In Gower, Lamb, Taylor, Willis and myself, we had players who could have got into most Test sides of the past and this knowledge unconsciously reinforced team morale for our second innings in Adelaide; the fact that we failed wasn't due to lack of leadership or shortage of the good old British bulldog spirit. Overall I still believed that we had the heart and the ability to take the smug smiles off a few faces. The people who thought that we were just a bunch of good blokes with no-one capable of applying the iron fist when it was necessary were wrong. When one or two looked a shade too casual in their approach, Willis quickly pulled them back into line.

I know it's not essential for a touring side to be happy among themselves, and that unhappy sides have won Test series; but it still helps if there is a good mix of personalities during the long and sometimes arduous months of travel. Players are flung together, sharing plane journeys, sharing hotel rooms, straining at practice and talking at team meetings. Any little ripples off the pitch will quickly show themselves out in the middle, but I can honestly say that Bob Willis's side was as harmonious as any I have played in. Some of these things were on my mind as I made my way from the hotel, across the beautiful Torrens River and into the Adelaide ground on the fourth morning of the Test. We were fully aware that only a disciplined performance occupying the crease for a day and a half would allow that morale-boosting draw.

When Lamb went cheaply, caught by Chappell off Yardley, I was in a position where I had to work out my own approach. Even though time was an important factor, I didn't believe that 6 hours at the crease scoring 30 runs would be of great value. I was determined to keep the scoreboard ticking and when Yardley pitched short, I gratefully accepted the chance to get off the mark with a 4 driven past point. Both Gower and myself were having trouble with Hogg, whose re-appearance back in a Test arena had given him an extra yard of pace and a refill of venom. Far from tailing off, here he was running in like a two-year-old in the heat with one of the most aggressive spells of fast bowling we had faced on the tour. Gower got a nasty crack on the shoulder when he ducked into one short-pitched delivery and twice I tried to hook and missed. The challenge was on. When I tried a big drive the ball spun back off my pad and fizzed dangerously close to my leg stump. Poor Hogg's face crumpled with frustration when, two balls later, I stretched my front foot across, clubbed him through extra cover for 4 and then flashed a big grin up the wicket. Sometimes fast bowlers must wish they had settled for a peaceful life selling life insurance. It can be heart-stopping at times, as Thomson discovered just a couple of overs later when I drove him to Hughes at extra cover. Australia's vice-captain grasped it at shoulder height, dropped it, caught it again and finally lost control. I didn't so much feel relief at the reprieve as anger at a stupid shot. 'Watch it, you idiot,' I swore to myself, and settled down to play through quietly to lunch.

Gower had gone into lunch at 88, offering further evidence of his arrival as a Test player of the highest class. There have been times when David has frustrated his followers with the apparent casualness of his approach, but this tour surely marked a turning point when he put his 'chancey' reputation to rest. A 4 after lunch, when Yardley over-pitched, took him into the nineties yet there could have been fewer cooler men on the ground as he headed for a fighting hundred. A couple of 2s off Yardley, a straight driven 3 and Gower had arrived on 99, at which point I prolonged his wait by pinching the bowling off the last ball of the over. We met in mid-wicket for a chat, but there's not much you can tell a batsman at such a critical stage, apart from offering the obvious encouragement. 'Don't give it away after all that hard work,' I told him with a big grin, and hoped he wasn't feeling the tension which was beginning to grip my legs.

I needn't have worried; when Thomson pitched one up on Gower's leg stump he pushed backward of square for the run which took him to his century. It had been a great effort and I imagined that along with the pleasure felt in the England dressing-room there was a growing conviction that we could save the Test. 'No way, no way must we lose,' I kept repeating. A 4 off Yardley gave me my fifty and put England ahead with 3 wickets down. Surely we couldn't make a mess of it for the second time in the innings? The answer wasn't long coming. Yardley pitched a fraction short, the sort of ball I look for, and I positioned myself to crack it away through cover. It bounced and turned, caught me in two minds and instead of pulling out of the shot, I sliced the ball head high to Dyson at deep point. England 236 for 4. Exit one angry batsman and suddenly we were back on the edge of the precipice with Lawson and the new ball appearing at our backs. In just over an hour and a half, immediately after tea, we lost 6 wickets for 57 runs, of which Lawson took 4 in 9 overs. Gower's epic came to an end when he glanced a Hogg delivery on to his leg stump and the rest fell nine, ten, jack. We were dismissed for 304, leaving Australia with the soft victory target of 83; not even the wicket of Wessels before stumps could lift our spirits. Australia lost just one more wicket the following morning before Dyson and Chappell steered them to a near-stranglehold 2 - 0 lead in the series.

Predictably, the Australian papers started to talk about an Ashes washout. We were told we were just not good enough and lacked the courage for a fight. This particular criticism hurt more than any other. When you are two-nil down with two to play, you tend to look closely at what has gone before, knowing there's no margin for error. I thought we'd got it right, but defeats in successive Tests put a question mark over the team. The only criticism I couldn't accept was that we had tossed away our chances without a fight at Adelaide. No-one who had been in the England dressing-room during our second innings collapse would have believed that we were throwing in the towel.

I went off to visit a sick boy in hospital on the afternoon after the end of the Test and later that evening I joined several team-mates for a drink. The pain of defeat was still there but I believed there was no point moping around before we moved off to Tasmania. A few of the players got up on to a chair to make toasts on the money I'd been handed by a London journalist, who had bet me that I wouldn't score 1000 Test runs in a calendar year, a mark I'd passed in the second innings at Adelaide. Vic Marks, my room-mate in Adelaide, relieved the disappointment which was still gnawing. 'I would like to make a toast to my Somerset colleague, Ian Botham,' he joked. 'He's collected fifty-odd Test caps for England . . . each one half a size bigger than the last.' It brought the house down and I was happy to join in the laughter. An England team which just a few hours before had been in despair was finding its spirit again. And never mind if the laughs were on me.

In the more relaxed atmosphere of Tasmania we massaged the bruises of defeat and planned our strategy for what had now become the most vital test of the tour, at Melbourne. I didn't play in the three-day game at Hobart, but David Gower took over the captaincy from Bob Willis and produced an England victory in an enterprising finish. Tasmania are now a formidable team in Sheffield Shield cricket, so there was plenty in the game, especially for the men whose Test places were still in the balance. Norman Cowans and Derek Pringle bowled well with the new ball, showing signs that they were taking notice of all the advice and encouragement coming their way. Geoff Cook and Graeme Fowler both made runs in each innings and thanks to a couple of declarations we raced home by 6 wickets. It was a good morale-boosting victory, but there was a disaster waiting just round the corner when we crossed to Launceston for a one-day game. The wicket they gave us was dreadful, especially when we were up against a fast bowler of Michael Holding's calibre. The West Indian gave Derek Randall the treatment and we were horrified when a short-pitched delivery ripped into his face, splitting his lip and breaking a bone just below his nose. Derek was in a bad way – I reckon that must have been the only time on tour when the little guy from Nottingham stopped talking. The rest of us didn't have much to say either; our 4-wicket victory couldn't compensate for the temporary loss of a player who had been one of the mainstays of the tour.

Randall, a one-off character, can infuriate opponents at times but, like Ian Gould, he can lift a team in one madcap moment. But here we were approaching Christmas and the Fourth Test with the Randall lip buttoned and stitched. It was a bad moment for all of us, although the arrival of the traditional Christmas Day festivities at the Melbourne Hilton took the pressure off for a few crazy hours. Robin Jackman was given the job of suggesting everybody's fancy dress outfit and some of his ideas were inspired. The skipper went as Napoleon, but I wasn't so sure about the choice with our possible Waterloo approaching at the Melbourne cricket ground twenty-four hours later. Norman Cowans went as another great athlete, Olympic champion Daley Thompson, while manager Doug Insole, 'the Inspector', appeared as Harvey Smith the showjumper. We wondered who he would most like to give a V-sign to. I went along as Sergeant Botham to Brigadier Jackman – does no-one want me as a captain any more? My greatest tactical triumph came later that afternoon when I eased a couple of pressmen, fully-clothed, into the swimming pool. It was a great day, but when the last toast had been drunk and we headed for an early night, our thoughts were dominated by the presence of the MCG just a couple of hundred yards away across the park.

Following our defeat in Adelaide, Bob Willis had taken off the kid gloves in his dealings with members of the team. Nothing nasty, but with our grip on the Ashes loosening he wanted the right response for a final, blinding push at the Australians. Derek Pringle was a case in point, a big, easy-going guy with a lot of untapped talent who had not always given the team what it wanted. 'This could be your last chance, so make the most of it,' he was told. Norman Cowans also figured highly in the pre-Test discussions; after being left out at Adelaide he had worked hard on his game and was perhaps in the right frame of mind to make a decisive effort. Bob was given a lot of criticism for his treatment of Cowans earlier in the tour and perhaps to an outsider it might have appeared strange. But inside the party the theory held that by making the going tough, the skipper was doing Cowans a favour.

I would imagine that training racehorses is much the same as bringing fast bowlers to a peak. If Norman had gone through the tour without making a single, telling contribution, the skipper could be accused of poor management. Willis had to gauge Cowans's mood more than his fitness. Walking from fine leg to third man in Brisbane might not have looked the best way of helping a young fast bowler, but I felt Willis wanted to know just what Cowans was made of. By the time we reached Melbourne I think he had a fair idea, and it was decided to bring him into the team, dropping a very disappointed Eddie Hemmings. The new Melbourne wicket, although something of an unknown quantity, would, we hoped, give greater help to the seam bowlers. It was likely to crack and perhaps produce inconsistent bounce, and if we had read it right there seemed more in it for the seamers than the spinners, as well as Hemmings had bowled in Adelaide.

We had kept our fingers crossed for Randall, but he was still feeling the effects of his facial injury, so we opened with Geoff Cook and Graeme Fowler, which pleased Chris Tavaré, who moved to No. 3 in the order. The Australians were claiming that they were clearly the better side in the series, but we still had our doubts about individuals and their collective ability to survive if we could put them under pressure, something we had been able to achieve only in brief moments during the previous three Tests. So often we had begun to take control only to toss away the advantage. This time we had to make sure that if we climbed the mountain we could stay there long enough to make it count. We had heard the strains of 'Waltzing Matilda' too often. Now it was time for a chorus of 'Land of Hope and Glory'. Our tactics were rammed home at the team meeting. We had to be positive. We had to be aggressive. Most of all, we had to win.

5

The Fourth Test, Melbourne

AS WE MADE OUR WAY past the early autographs hunters on the walk to the magnificent Melbourne Cricket Ground, not even the most dizzy-eyed dreamer among us would have suggested we were heading for one of the greatest Test finishes of all time. Over the next five days – there was no rest day – my emotions were tossed on a roller-coaster of tension before that heart-fluttering finish at 12.24 on Thursday, 30 December. I try to inject excitement into my life by flying aircraft and racing motor cars, but nothing could compete with the fourth Test of the 1982/3 series. It was classic, building towards a final confrontation which drained me both mentally and physically, a memory to warm me in old age and provide many a tale over a Sunday lunchtime pint. It stretched us all from start to finish. In the England dressing-room, in those anxious minutes before the first over, I could sense a greater urgency among the team. Some of the banter and bravado was missing as we all focused our minds on a match which we knew we must not lose if we wanted to keep a hand on the Ashes. I think we were all determined to bust a gut to level the score.

I watched the skipper on our television monitor as he went out for the toss with Greg Chappell. Bob Willis called 'Heads'; it came down the other way and Chappell unhesitatingly put us in to bat. The Melbourne authorities had chosen a wicket which had not been used before. It looked firm and crusty with a few bare patches, but underneath the surface there was a fair amount of moisture. 'It's an unknown quantity, but I'm hopeful our fast bowlers will get us away to a good start,' Chappell told the television viewers. I thought Bob looked a bit downhearted when he agreed that there was likely to be some early life in the wicket.

The first ball of the fourth Test was bowled by Lawson to Geoff Cook.

Norman Cowans, a study in concentration during the Fourth Test, for which he was named Man of the Match.

How could it have missed? I thought I'd got David Hookes leg before in the Fourth Test.

Above A short-pitched delivery to Kim Hughes neatly evaded and *below* even I couldn't stare the wicket into falling down.

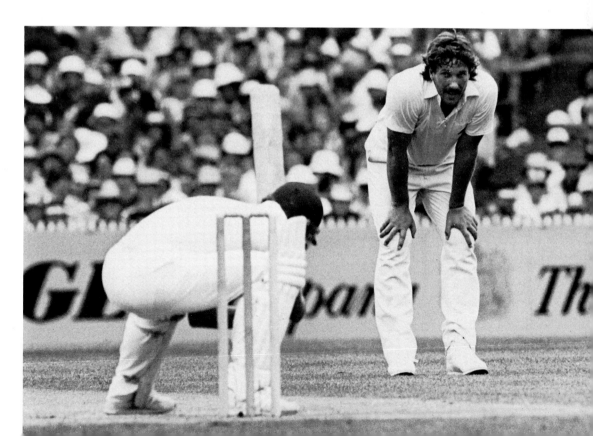

Bob Willis appealing for Kim Hughes's wicket, also in the Fourth Test; he was
given not out, but eventually the England skipper collected.

Self with Geoff Miller and Bob Taylor running to congratulate Norman
Cowans on getting Kepler Wessels's wicket in the Fourth Test.

Appealing for David Hookes's wicket caught behind when he was on 37 in his second innings in the Fourth Test. He was given not out.

Norman Cowans giving a big lbw shout against Allan Border during the
Fourth Test.

Jubilation as Jeff Thomson's wicket finally falls in the Fourth Test, with Australia needing only 3 runs to win the Ashes. *Left* with Derek Pringle; *below* with Bob Willis.

More than twenty-five playing hours later, I bowled the last ball of the match to Jeff Thomson. What went on in between produced one of the most enthralling matches in Test history. Don't ever let anyone tell you Test cricket is dead. This game overshadowed everything else on the tour. One-day matches are marvellous fun but in terms of satisfaction – for player and for spectator, I think – comparing them with Tests is like comparing take-away chicken with a banquet. Few people outside the England dressing-room had much faith in our new opening partnership and the Australians clearly had memories of Cook's dismissal at Perth, when they crowded him with two close catchers on the leg side. Cook's method against the moving ball was to get on the back foot, but he didn't look comfortable and was soon hit a painful blow in the groin by Lawson. It was Fowler who was first to go, though, when he got square on to Hogg, the ball took the outside edge and Chappell made a fine diving catch at first slip.

The sun was shining, there wasn't a cloud in the sky, yet the amount of moisture in the wicket prompted the Australian bowlers to call for sawdust on their footholds. It was a strange sight and it didn't make us feel any easier as we watched the gripping first session. Chappell clearly had his own thoughts about the wicket and by bringing on Yardley after an hour no doubt hoped to exploit the dampness. Our interest pricked up immediately; all our reckoning had been that if the wicket did crack it would probably produce variable bounce and give greater help to the seam bowlers. We had wanted to bowl first ourselves and it was perhaps fortunate that neither Lawson nor Thomson did well in the opening session. Both pitched too short when a fuller length on a seaming wicket could have had us in all sorts of trouble. As it was, things were bad enough when Cook departed at 25 to a ball wide of the off stump from Thomson, who had given us all a laugh at the start of the match when he appeared looking a lot more youthful thanks to a blond rinse in his hair. Cook, though, had no time to notice things like that as he initially moved back, then attempted to drive and was badly balanced when he edged the ball to the ever-so-safe hands of Chappell. It was Greg's 111th catch for Australia, an all-time record, beating Bobby Simpson – and the man with the safest pair of slip hands in the world had a smile on his face which seemed to stretch from one side of the cavernous MCG to the other.

In our dressing-room, where we had been praying for a good start, gloom set in. No-one had talked much on tour about the banned South African rebels, but in the dull hush I wondered how many of us were thinking about the impact Graham Gooch might have made on this series. For the moment, though, we had to do the best with what we had which, as far as the chanting, near-capacity Melbourne crowd was concerned, wasn't much. Melbourne can be the most intimidating ground in the world, especially for an out-of-form batsman, and Tavaré's temperament was very much on trial as he fought to counter the hysterical support for Thomson and the barracking against his own unfair reputation as the Canterbury snail. For light relief, after Tavaré had played Thomson to third man for 3, they unfurled a banner proclaiming, 'Hey, Tavaré, what's the rush?' Black humour, indeed.

Part of our strategy for the match had been to attack Yardley because we didn't want Chappell using him as a stock bowler for three-quarters of the day while the seamers took a rest. If we could fill our boots against the off-spinner, Chappell would have far less room for manoeuvre. Tavaré, throwing off his recent poor form, was our man for the occasion after David Gower had gone, edging Hogg to Rod Marsh. Yardley's first over after lunch cost him 10 runs as Tavaré lofted him through mid-on and then whipped a full toss off his legs for another boundary. In Yardley's next over, Tavaré took three more boundaries and, with Lamb going well at the other end, we were on top of the Australian attack, imposing our aggression, for perhaps the first time in the series. At tea we had reached 180-odd, and 200 came up soon afterwards; we were climbing the mountain again, but could we stay there this time? Yardley made sure we didn't as he leapt across to take yet another great catch in the gully, giving Thomson the chance to gesture Tavaré back to the pavilion. And just 10 runs later, Yardley was the bowler when Lamb swung off the front foot straight to Dyson at long on. I'm sure if Lamb had studied the replay on the Melbourne scoreboard he might have come to the conclusion that maybe it wasn't the wisest shot to attempt in the circumstances. Both he and Tavaré had departed in the eighties and the big dipper of a Test had taken another sudden plunge.

I was determined not to let the tempo slacken, hitting a Yardley top spinner through square cover for 4. When Yardley pitched a fraction short, I pulled him in front of square for 4, then cut him over point to the fence and drove the next ball off the back foot through cover for another boundary. I was enjoying the situation and another pulled 4 from the final ball of Yardley's next over took me into the mid-twenties. But that was about as far as I got because when Yardley managed a fraction of turn, I checked my shot and clipped the ball into the hands of Wessels at short leg. Once again I had started confidently and then thrown it away just when I was fancying myself for a big score. Like Lamb I could have studied my dismissal on the Melbourne scoreboard – sixty-five thousand fans were having a good look – but I just couldn't bring myself to glance up from the ground. For the moment it was bad enough being out and knowing I'd let the Aussies off the hook. A few runs later Miller was given out, caught at point by Border off the bowling of Yardley, but I had my doubts about that decision when I saw it again on the television replay.

We managed only 284 all out and knowing another 60 or 100 could have been decisive, we were not pleased with our position. Our total was reasonable yet so much still depended on the performance of the wicket, and of our bowlers, who needed to show a lot of discipline to exploit the variable bounce. The new strip was certainly better than some of the recent wickets at the MCG, but in my view there was still room for improvement; maybe the money which was invested by the sponsors in the scoreboard might have been better spent on the wicket.

I wasn't managing much swing with the new ball – the Australian Kookaburras never seem to suit me in that respect – and after 3 overs I gave way to Cowans in a pre-arranged move which produced a stunning pay-off. Unlike the rest of us who were under strict orders to bowl to plan, trying wherever possible to restrict scoring and tax the patience of the batsmen, Cowans was given his head. The chains were being taken off and after the morale-bruising experiences at Perth and Brisbane, Norman was told, in effect, that now he was on his own and it was up to him what he made of the chance. For 15 deliveries, 2 of which shot venomously over Dyson's head, Cowans was threatening but expensive. From the sixteenth delivery, Dyson played half forward, missed a ball nipping back at him and was trapped leg before. Nice one, Norm! When Greg Chappell came to the wicket, still in the frame of mind where he was determined to attack from the word go, the fact that the first ball was going to be delivered by the rookie of the England attack seemed to stiffen the arrogance of his stride. I watched the action from second slip; the scene looked like something out of one of my favourite Westerns. Chappell looked at Cowans with what seemed like open contempt: even the carefully-placed ambush of leg slip, forward short leg, deep square and fine leg couldn't deter him from picking up the challenge. He sipped a drink from the trolley, asked for his guard, took a moment to look around the field and then settled down to face Cowans. It was a few minutes after high noon. The ball was short and so, too, was Chappell's patience as he hooked high towards square leg where Allan Lamb had to move no more than a couple of yards before hugging the ball to his chest with all the coolness of a man who might have been catching a rubber ball on the beach. Chappell, the prize gunfighter, had been beaten to the draw and the kid Cowans was slapping every palm in sight. It was an important wicket for him and for the team; suddenly our self-esteem soared.

Wessels, half the player when the ball is pitched on or around leg stump, was bowled off his pads and then Border obliged me by attempting a rather airy drive which went through the gap to hit his middle stump. It was a good morning's work which might have been even better had the decision gone my way when I rapped Hughes on the pads early in his innings. It was a mighty close thing and, when Hookes was given a dubious leg before let-off midway through the afternoon, my faith in Australian umpires started to waver again. The partnership between Hughes and Hookes produced an interesting contrast with two basically attacking players pursuing different roles to guide Australia back into calmer waters. Hughes subdued his natural instincts to push the fight to England, settling instead for a controlled innings in which he took as few chances as possible. Hookes, highly regarded by England as the major threat behind Chappell, maintained a flamboyant approach, refusing to let his mistakes inhibit him in any way. He plays the way he enjoys and when he makes a false shot he invariably follows with a great stroke off the next ball.

Hookes reached his half-century before aiming another ambitious drive at Pringle and giving Taylor a straightforward catch behind the stumps. 'Any wicket for medium-pacer Pringle at this level is a bonus,' wrote Peter McFarline in the following morning's *Melbourne Age* and while that assessment would have been fair in the early stages, I thought that Pringle's improvement was one of the bonuses of the tour. He got better the longer the tour progressed and watching him perform at Melbourne made me think that perhaps he had been underbowled. He has a lot of ability and I hope that people will leave him alone and allow his natural talent to develop in good time.

By mid-afternoon, Australia had progressed past 250 for the loss of 5 wickets; our chances of getting back into contention for the Ashes were finely balanced. We realized that if we trailed by too many on the first innings, Australia were unlikely to be tested on a wearing wicket when they came to bat again. It was a time when everyone had to keep their nerve and Willis, despite the first signs of a stomach bug which was to affect him for the rest of the match, provided a cool head in a crisis. He whipped out Hughes and a belligerent Marsh before Miller stepped in to torment the tail-enders and leave us facing a first innings deficit of just 3 runs. Not a bad day's work, we reckoned, as we made for an early night to recharge the batteries and face another day on the roller-coaster.

The MCG wicket was still giving the batsmen cause for suspicion but our only option was to adopt a positive approach when we batted again, and luckily we were helped by a fair amount of short-pitched bowling, especially from Thomson and Lawson. Hogg, realizing the value of bowling straight, was the danger as the game swung back and forth towards its marvellous climax.

After nearly an hour's play we were 40 without loss and looking good. Twenty minutes later we were 45 for 3 with Cook, Tavaré and Gower all back in the pavilion. Fowler held things together with a gritty innings, but Hogg struck after lunch with 2 wickets in 4 balls and suddenly we were back on the rack at 129 for 5. Neither side was able to gain a clear advantage as we went at each other like old-fashioned fairground fighters. I struck a few useful blows with 8 boundaries, but then got my nose bloodied when I flashed at Thomson and sent the ball straight to Chappell at slip. Taylor and Pringle showed a fair bit of resilience, but our hearts sank again when umpire Tony Crafter was sure that a rising delivery from Thomson would have hit Taylor's stumps after striking him on the pad.

We had the benefit of television replays in the dressing-room and groaned as we watched playbacks which, we believed, showed the ball would have cleared the stumps by a few inches. But Crafter was in the best position of all, I suppose, and the fact that millions of television viewers across the world had the advantage of slow-motion replays only increased the pressure on him. At Melbourne, with the giant scoreboard and numerous television cameras watching every decision in detail, I wondered whether the umpires had many sleepless nights. Taylor's decision appeared to be wrong, but there seemed greater injustice earlier in the day when Gower had been given out when he swung at – and surely missed – a short-pitched delivery from Lawson which Marsh took down the leg side. The slips made a big song and dance about it but Marsh himself didn't seem too convinced and often that can be the best guide of all. So we were left with a second innings total of 294, which gave Australia two days in which to score 292 for victory and put the Ashes out of our reach. I thought we were the slight favourites because while most of the Australian batsmen were in reasonable form, their recent record of chasing runs in the last innings of a Test had not been impressive; and over-riding everything were their fears about the condition of the wicket. In the event, the wicket didn't play much of a part in the fourth day drama which took this Test into the classic class. Both teams were trying to make things happen rather than wait for their opponent to make mistakes and so produced a game in which courage and fist-clenched determination became its key qualities.

Bob Willis, ignoring the overcast conditions which might have helped me to swing the ball, opted to open the attack with Norman Cowans. As it turned out he made the right decision, but no-one could have forecast the startling results which would be achieved in the momentous day ahead. Cowans had wanted the new ball in his hands from the start of the tour and now he was being given the chance to prove himself worthy of it. All the miserable moments of the tour, the times when he perhaps believed he was not being given a fair chance to succeed, had to be put to the back of his mind as he paced out his run-up and prepared to bowl to Dyson. Ten other England players, plus those watching in the dressing-room, were willing him to give it a real go and Cowans was in no mood to let them down. The Australian batsmen, most especially Greg Chappell, had been treating Cowans like a gawky kid at his first party, but now he could show them that he had come through the harrowing experiences of his early Test matches and was ready to claim a place at the top table. Dyson and Wessels might have had other ideas but this time the tempo of their opening lacked conviction as Cowans put on an extra yard of pace. Wessels, lucky to survive when a ball kept low and shot through his defence to race for 4 byes, slashed a shortish delivery through the hands of Tavaré at third slip, but even that demoralizing loss couldn't keep Cowans down. In his fifth over, a ball pitched up around leg stump beat Wessels and bowled him off his pads. Thirty-seven for 1 and we all raced towards mighty Norman to slap his palms in celebration of the breakthrough we sorely needed to keep the pressure on the Australian batsmen, in particular Chappell, who was arriving at the wicket on a 'king pair'. The Australian captain had apparently given orders that morning for his batsmen to attack whenever possible; and he was obviously heeding his own advice when he attempted to clip his first ball from Cowans off his legs and managed to send it through the hands of Geoff Cook at short leg. It was a hard chance, sure enough, but there was nothing we wouldn't have given at that moment for another Chappell first-ball duck. Cowans sunk to his knees while the rest of us wondered whether we would get a second chance before Chappell got into his stride.

The answer wasn't long in coming; Chappell had made only a couple of runs when he tried to drive Cowans off his back foot and sent the ball climbing into the covers. For a few moments there was a still silence over the ground, split only by an expletive from Chappell. We all seemed mesmerized as the ball headed for Ian Gould, fielding as substitute for Graeme Fowler who had cracked a bone in his big right toe while batting the previous day. It is at moments like these that Test matches are won and lost and here was Gould, one of the characters of the tour who had kept spirits high, staring at perhaps the most crucial chance of the series. He dived low and left, clutching the catch close to the ground before bouncing up and into the arms of David Gower, his fists thrashing above his head. If I had to pick a high spot of the tour this was probably it . . . the Cockney 'keeper and the young man from Jamaica combining to defeat Chappell and, in the process, sending a surge of spirit and energy through the rest of the team. We just had to win now, we thought, and when Dyson surrendered to a marvellous diving catch by Tavaré before lunch, the odds were firmly in our favour.

Dyson's wicket came at a good moment for me because it allowed an answer to the near forty-thousand crowd who had been giving me a fair bit of stick during the morning session. When the replay of Dyson's dismissal came up on the screen above the stand, I happily pointed up to the pictures of the Australian opener edging a ball which had moved away from him in the air. The Melbourne crowd booed and I gestured back to them . . . it was fairly good-natured but I could sense that the tension was growing as much round the field as it was in the middle. The crowd at the MCG appreciated the intensity of the struggle and although things didn't go Australia's way in the morning session, I was impressed by the way they got behind Cowans. There was clearly a lot of sympathy for him around the ground and it didn't take long for the banners of support to unfurl over the advertising hoardings.

A match which had swung one way and then the other for more than four days might have been sealed irretrievably in our favour when Geoff Miller twice beat a tentative Hookes shortly before lunch. David Gower couldn't hold on to the first chance at silly point and then I just failed to reach an edge at slip. The fates, it appeared, didn't want this titanic struggle to end so soon and it was Hookes, together with Hughes, who set about re-building the barricades around Australia's Ashes hopes during an afternoon when little went right for us.

I had a big appeal for a catch behind the wicket when Hookes was on 37, but umpire Rex Whitehead was not impressed. Then I hit Hughes on the front pad and Whitehead again turned down the shout for leg before. Hughes edged the next ball down to the third-man boundary and Willis, spotting my anger, quickly raced over to tell me to calm down. It was fair enough comment: I had allowed myself to overheat at what I thought were two doubtful decisions, though the skipper maybe needed to take his own advice when he believed Hookes had edged a catch to Bob Taylor. Hookes responded by taking three 4s and a 3 off Willis. At 170 for 3, Australia were taking control again. Then, within 3 runs, both Hughes and Hookes had departed: Hughes to a great diving catch by Taylor and Hookes to a fabulous effort from the skipper, whose bout of gastric 'flu had reached a debilitating peak on the fourth day. He managed only 9 overs, felt giddy and sick, yet refused to leave the field while the game was balanced so finely. And here he was, running furiously from mid-on and taking a catch over his head when Hookes failed to connect cleanly with a short-pitched ball from Cowans.

In a matter of minutes, the anxiety which was beginning to squeeze our concentration had been washed away and now the tide was flowing back in our favour as Cowans made his second major contribution to the day's play. He accounted for Marsh and then Yardley, bowled by one of the few balls which misbehaved off the wicket, before catching Lawson at fine leg and then trapping Hogg leg before. Australia were 218 for 9, still 74

David Gower, keeping England going in the Fifth Test in Sydney.

Greg Chappell scoring off Norman Cowans in the Fifth Test.

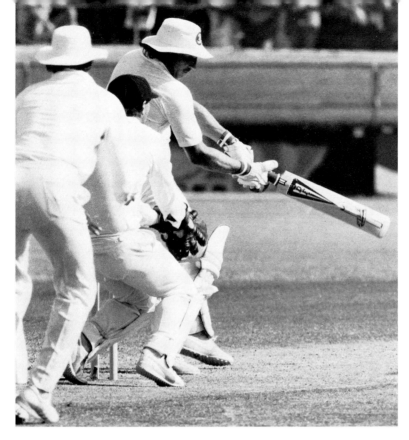

Having a go in the Fifth Test, with Rodney Marsh and Greg Chappell in close attendance.

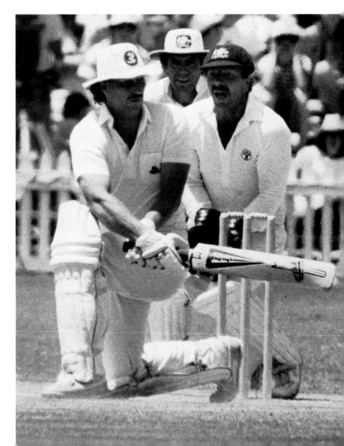

Geoff Lawson, the Australian fast bowler, who was named Man of the Series.

runs away from victory with two men at the wicket, Border and Thomson, whose previous batting form in the series had been so wretched you wouldn't have bet a brass farthing on their survival. But Border is a fighter who, in a crisis, finally found the inspiration to put his miserable summer behind him and play with the courage and competence which every England player knew he could have produced at any moment in the series. We were lucky that it had taken until Melbourne for Border to recapture the confidence eroded by a succession of low scores during recent Test matches. Thomson, his partner, could also be an awkward customer if he could smell any sort of challenge in the air. When the situation didn't suit him, he would go for the slog like a man who couldn't disguise his agitation at batting No. 11 in the order. On this occasion, though, his antenna clearly picked up the signals that a few heroics were in order if Australia were to turn the odds around one last time.

We quickly had to decide fresh tactics which would give us greater hopes of success. We could attack both the out-of-touch Border and the more vulnerable Thomson all the time, or else deny Border as much of the strike as possible and try to concentrate our efforts against Thomson. We decided on the latter course, but with Border beginning to farm the bowling effectively, the opportunities we had of bowling at Jeff were curtailed. After days of hard fighting, no-one was going to lay down and die, especially with the Ashes in sight for Australia and a series to save for England. Now it was all or nothing, the final moments when a great Test put on its last, heart-thumping act with two Australians holding the hopes of a nation in their hands. Slowly, run by run, Thomson and Border inched along the road to glory while England laboured to hold them back. Thoughts of a champagne celebration began to recede. Three quarters of an hour after being in a position where we thought we couldn't lose, we knew that every run scored raised the tension on the field another notch, testing our resolve to contain their daring last effort. Ten, twenty, thirty runs; would Australia work a miracle? There was no panic but the anxious faces betrayed the intensity of the fight. Surely we couldn't come so far and then end up losing the Ashes like this? Concentration was total as everyone strained still harder to save the runs which were building the confidence of both batsmen to a point where Border looked like the player of old and Thomson attacked and defended with what seemed to us contemptuous ease.

It seemed the game couldn't possibly hold any more surprises – but the skies opened up a few minutes before six. The people of Melbourne who had seen little but drought for months couldn't believe it, and neither could we. Australia had cut the deficit to 46 runs and for thirty minutes, as the rain came down, both teams took a much-needed break from the supercharged atmosphere. The Australians, we knew, would be rather less anxious than us, for already Border and Thomson had done a great job without a trace of distress. So far we had failed to disturb them and although we saw no reason to change our tactics, the usual bustle of the dressing-room was missing as we waited for the sun to dry off the wicket surrounds sufficiently for us to re-start. There was time for Australia to add another 9 runs and take the Test to the brink before the close of play. Who would now apply the final push?

I felt totally exhausted as I made my way back to our hotel that night. Mentally, the day had been very wearing and it wasn't long before I turned in. Sleep didn't come easily. So many things went through my mind as I re-played incidents which had shaped the course of the game. What if Hookes had gone early – or been given out caught behind when Australia were struggling towards a recovery? What if Gould had dropped that catch and given Chappell another life? The picture I tried to force out of my mind was the one of a jubilant Border and Thomson being chaired off the field in triumph. I was sure Bob Willis was having similar agonies that night, knowing that if the tactics failed, or a little bit of luck went against him, he would be remembered as another captain who had lost the Ashes. I didn't sleep well, but I'm sure Bob had a more restless night as he waited to get to grips with the Australian batsmen. Even the knowledge that in a century of Ashes cricket no team had scored so many for the last wicket to win a Test match could not have brought much respite.

I skipped breakfast, apart from a single cup of tea, preferring to feed off the adrenalin which was already causing me to hurry through my normally calm ritual in the hours before the start of a day's play. Kathy gave me a good luck kiss while she pondered whether to stay away from the ground in case her presence brought disaster to the team. Sometimes she worries that she'll bring me bad luck, though it's a superstition I don't share, especially when I'm doing well! I checked that my gold talisman was in place around my neck. I'm sure the same kind of rituals were being repeated in other rooms throughout the Hilton Hotel – and probably among the opposition, too – before the players gathered in the foyer for the two-hundred-yard walk to the ground. All of us were feeling the pressure; it was so strong you could reach out your hand and touch it. You could sense from the animated conversations that while everyone was trying to appear unconcerned, stomachs were churning with tension.

An hour before the start of play, thousands were streaming into the ground knowing that the first ball could also be the last. Around eighteen thousand spectators made it to the MCG that morning; I heard later that in the final minutes before the great battle got under way, grown men were seen running from all corners of the park to make sure they didn't miss the first delivery. In both dressing-rooms, smiles were like gold dust; tension gripped everyone in the moments when the players followed the umpires out into the middle. High up on the terraces, a lone bugler played the Last Post. We took up the attack with Australia needing 37 runs to clinch the Ashes. We were still favourites to take the last wicket, but in the opening overs neither Thomson nor Border gave any reason for optimism.

Thomson almost taunted us by taking 18 of the first 24 deliveries, batting with huge assurance. He was actually enjoying a situation in which a tail-ender, whose batting normally had the life expectancy of a kamikaze pilot, was playing a match-winning role and playing it well. There was no panic, the running between the wickets was well-judged and with each single or scampered 2 our hope of victory diminished. The skipper conceded 4 runs off his first 4 overs; Cowans bowled 3 successive maidens before taking the new ball after half an hour, with Australia 33 runs from the Ashes. It was sweaty palms time, believe me, and although we could have switched tactics and attacked Border as well as Thomson, it was decided to allow Border the single at the start of an over because we still fancied our chances against the genuine tail-ender. That genuine tail-ender didn't give us much encouragement as he carved Willis off his stumps wide of point for 3. It brought up the fifty partnership and cut the victory target to 23. Then Border pushed forward off the last ball of that over, raced off for a single, and made his ground as Lamb and Gould fumbled and collided in hasty confusion. At any other time it would have had us falling about. Now the rest of us tried to hide our despair. Twenty-two wanted.

Cowans, whose 6 wickets had given his bowling a new air of confidence, stood up remarkably well to the tension of those opening overs. He was getting very little response from the wicket, but his accuracy ensured that neither batsman was being given easy runs. The crowd were enthralled, cheering every single, applauding Thomson when he met the ball in the middle of the bat and booing us when we cut off a boundary. I'm sure you could have stood outside the ground and known exactly what was going on just by listening. Every so often, in the brief silences, I could hear that bugler rallying Australia to victory.

The cheers crescendoed again when Border pushed Cowans to short extra cover and Gould couldn't reach the ball quickly enough from his deep position to prevent the batsmen going through for 2. It gave Border his half-century and cut the difference to 20 runs. As I looked around at the rest of the team I could read the message that we were fighting for our lives, a message which the scoreboard hammered home after Border had swung Cowans away to fine leg for a single. 'Australia needs 19 runs to win the Ashes,' it flashed repeatedly, but we didn't need telling a second time. Getting the target below 20 was a major achievement for Australia and a great psychological boost for them; it was probably the reason for a double bowling change. I replaced the skipper and then he took over from Cowans for what we imagined would be our very last chance of staying in the fight.

I have been in some pretty tight situations before and I have always enjoyed the sensation, but this time I could feel my stomach churning as Australia crept ever closer to their target. Border kept out my first 4 deliveries and then took a single to Cowans at third man off the fifth. Eighteen wanted and Thomson was facing the last ball of the over. 'Come on, Both, knock the rabbit over,' I was saying to myself as I walked back to my mark. But the rabbit wasn't having any of it and Thomson earned another big cheer by keeping out a ball pitched on off stump.

Having decided to stick to our tactics we could only hold our course. Bob Willis was offering encouragement whenever he could, but other than keep Border quiet he was gambling on Thomson making a mistake; whether that was brought about by over-confidence or lack of technique didn't matter. With no pressure on him, Border had played himself out of his bad run, so increasingly we knew that unless we nailed Jeff we would lose the Test. For Border there was no-one at slip and when the skipper strayed a fraction outside off stump, the ball was lofted to third man for 2 more runs. Sixteen wanted . . . and then 14, as Border scampered through for 2 after playing Willis to square leg. When the drinks came on after an hour's play, most of us felt so drained it was a struggle to get a glass to our lips. The match had been swinging one way and then the other for five days and we all knew that in the next half-hour both it and the Ashes contest would be settled with awful finality. The winners' tactics would be justified and the torment would be forgotten; for the losers there would only be the deadening feeling of failure which comes when you have been knocked down in the last round. We turned back towards the middle. There was no bell, no call for 'seconds out' but for the last time I heard the bugler on the terraces; then the notes were drowned by the wild applause for Thomson when he stepped away to square leg and cut me for 2 runs to third man, repeating the shot for a single two balls later. Eleven wanted, then 10 as Thomson took a run to cover off the next over from Willis.

In all honesty we'd thought Australia didn't stand a chance of getting the runs when they'd lost their ninth wicket the previous evening, but now they were so close to achieving their goal that the turnabout almost took the stuffing out of me as I prepared to bowl my third over of the morning. Thomson slashed and missed at the second delivery and I think all of Australia missed a heartbeat as the ball flew harmlessly through to Taylor. 'Give us a tickle next time, mate,' I shouted down the wicket and two balls later Thomson obliged, sending an edge dangerously close to Tavaré at second slip, from where it skidded down to third man for a single. Nine runs needed; Border's response to the chanting of his name by the crowd was to drive the final ball of the over through extra cover for 3. Now the margin was 6 runs . . . maybe one shot or a couple of edges. How could Australia fail after coming so far? Would we get a last chance of bowling at Thomson? These were the things racing through my mind as Border glanced Willis square for two runs and then played out the remaining four balls of the over with ease.

Four runs to win, 3 to tie and 'Two runs to play with' said the skipper as he threw me the ball for the eighteenth over of the morning. I was scared stiff for about the first time on a cricket pitch as I waited at the end of my run-up while Thomson settled himself. What sort of ball should I aim to deliver? Thomson had looked vulnerable outside the offstump, but so far that morning he had got away with it by giving himself room to play airily at anything wide of the wicket. But if I didn't try to tempt him and give myself a hope of a catch behind the wicket, he would almost certainly content himself just with defending a straight delivery. I was sure Jeff was going through a similar sort of torment. For him the question was whether to go for a single and give his senior partner the chance to finish things off. I gave the ball, now 12 overs old, a final rub on my pants and came striding in with the intention of playing Thomson at his own game, baiting him with a ball pitched around off stump.

It was wider than I wanted, Jeff sensed it was there to hit, but his decision seemed to fail him and a shot which had started out as a slash fell away into an unconvincing stab. It seemed that at the last second his nerve wavered. The ball took the outside edge and the crowd watched in mesmerized horror as it flew towards Tavaré at second slip. Some of the other players told me later that they had turned their heads away when they saw the ball jump out of Chris's hands and so missed Geoff Miller's dash from first slip to clasp the chance in both hands. Poor Border said afterwards that his heart jumped in his mouth three times as first he thought the ball had gone for 4, then he saw it slip in and out of Tavaré's hands before Miller finally grabbed it. Thomson told me he had tried to guide the ball for a single 'instead of giving it a bloody good thump'. Although he'd provided me with my 100th Test wicket against Australia, I was much too excited to realize it at the time.

We ran from the field with our fists punching out victory salutes but as soon as we were back in the dressing-room reaction to the effort hit everyone at the same time. Players slumped into chairs, peering at the ceiling and not saying a word: anyone coming in at that moment might have thought they had walked into the losers' dressing-room. For maybe a minute, no-one spoke as we slowly let the thrill of victory restore the energy to our muscles and clear the numbness from our brains. Then I reached into my bag for a big celebration cigar. The only sound in the room was of the match striking the box and flaring into life. I waited and blew rings slowly across the room. 'Okay. So who can take pressure?' I enquired.

Only then were we ready for the champagne and the delirious celebrations of success. Nothing was going to stop us having a little bit of fun before catching the afternoon flight to Sydney. If nothing else went our way on tour, at least we'd carry home the knowledge of a great Test played for England. We were supposed to be second-rate, we were reckoned to be gutless . . . but we'd proved we were no pushovers in one of the most exciting Test finishes of all time. What we had to do now was to repeat the performance in the fifth and deciding Test; but no-one was thinking about that as the champagne corks flew.

6

The Fifth Test, Sydney

WITHIN A COUPLE OF HOURS of Australia losing their last wicket and with it the Melbourne Test, we were packing our bags for the flight to Sydney and the final confrontation of the series. The tour itinerary gave us just a few days between Tests, but such was the mood of the party after tasting triumph in Melbourne that no-one seemed to be concerned yet that our minds and energies must be channelled into one last effort. The smoke of the fourth Test battle was still hanging in the air and our departure from Melbourne was a riot with Allan Lamb parading around the hotel foyer in a joke mask and other players horsing about. Even Chris Tavaré, who had initially dropped Thomson before Geoff Miller snatched at the chance, could smile about the incident. 'It was all pre-planned, Both, didn't anybody tell you?' he beamed. The victory had lifted our spirits to a point where we believed the pressure was now on Australia to keep their nerve if they hoped to retain their 2–1 advantage and pocket the Ashes in Sydney. We felt ready for anything they could throw at us. Just to make sure the point wasn't lost on Greg Chappell and Co., Bob Willis rather mischievously claimed, 'We have seen Australia collapse under pressure before and if we can get them in that situation again, I'm sure we can win this Test.' Chappell, I read in my morning paper, wasn't impressed. 'It's psychological warfare. It's all bulldust,' he said. 'We've been the better side in the series – they've been the ones who have folded more times than us.'

So the fifth Test was warming up nicely off the field even though it clearly wasn't hot enough for one Sydney journalist who sought to build a confrontation between Rodney Hogg and myself on New Year's Eve. The first I knew about it was a phone call from the England manager at the house I was sharing in a Sydney suburb with my wife and her parents. An Australian newspaper, I was told, had carried a story that two players had been involved in a fracas and English papers, following up the tale, had named Hogg and myself as the culprits. I was staggered; apart from wishing Hogg a Happy New Year an hour before midnight, I hadn't seen him all evening. It seemed to me that both of us had been victims of Scribe's Law. A journalist had simply picked on an Australian player who had something of a volatile reputation and teamed him with I. T. Botham, always fair game. Once they had the names, the story wrote itself, of course.

For the record, I had gone to the Pier One Tavern on Sydney's waterfront along with my wife and in-laws. Several other England players and their wives were also invited by the Tavern management so a party of around two dozen squeezed on to three or four tables. It was New Year's Eve and we were all enjoying ourselves, along with about five hundred celebrating Australians, some of whom were members of the Test team in a separate part of the bar. At one point a television crew arrived asking to film our party, but when they were told that it was a private occasion which we wanted to keep that way they politely moved away from us. Then a photographer asked me to pose for a picture with one or two of the Australians, and although it meant an awkward scramble through chairs and tables I reluctantly agreed if it meant the cameraman would then move off to his own celebrations. No-one was falling about, no-one was looking for trouble and how an arm around Hogg's shoulder could be made to appear like a brawl beats me. I was supposed to have tweaked Hogg's ear, causing him to round on me and square up for a fight which was averted only by the intervention of other England players.

I suppose anyone reading the story would have believed that 'blasted Botham' was at it again, but nothing could have been further from the truth and I didn't appreciate the publicity. I don't mind being ribbed for things I've done, but I don't think it's at all funny when stories cross the borderline between fact and fiction. When I finally finish with cricket, I want to be remembered for the way I played, not for the way I'm supposed to have brawled off the pitch. The Pier One episode put a cloud over my mental build-up to the final Test. It takes a lot to upset or depress me, but I can honestly say that the false reports of trouble with Hogg put me in the worst possible frame of mind for a vital Test match. Instead of concentrating on my contribution to the Ashes decider, my thoughts and my time were taken up by talks with my London solicitor. The time in Sydney, one of the world's most beautiful and exciting cities, should have been perfect for my family and myself; instead it became a terrible strain.

All the usual preparations went ahead, though the morning net practice on New Year's Day was an event of particular significance for Derek Randall, who had had the stitches removed from his upper lip and needed to reassure everyone that his confidence had not been shattered by the incident with Michael Holding in Tasmania.

We were lucky enough to have the services of several net bowlers, including Surrey's Dave Thomas and Hampshire's Kevin Emery, who were playing grade cricket in Sydney, and they helped to give Randall quite a lively time. They were told to bowl short, testing his reaction against the bouncer and, although Derek was typically chirpy afterwards, I thought he had looked a trifle shaky when the ball was getting up around his ears, understandably. A decision would have to be made whether to risk Randall against an Australian pace attack which would be certain to seek out any doubts in his mind. Our options were limited though, and if Derek were left out we would have to risk Trevor Jesty straight after his arrival from England. But we knew Randall was a real fighter who wouldn't be a bad bloke to have around if things got tight and a little heated over the next few days. Our other batting problem centred around Graeme Fowler, still in considerable pain after fracturing his big right toe in Melbourne; a short period in the nets convinced us that he wouldn't stand up to a five-day Test.

Geoff Cook was still feeling his bruised ribs, but announced himself fit enough to play; that left us with no option but to restore Tavaré to open the innings with him, something Tavaré was reluctant to do after his success in the first innings at Melbourne where he batted at No. 3. He had been hoping to stay in a position where he seemed to play with more fluency. Chris took a lot of stick both from the spectators and some of the Australian commentators, but there were several occasions on tour when he showed his true ability, and I remained convinced that if he can just put a harder streak into his game he will become a very fine Test player. The responsibility of opening the innings puts his talent into a straight jacket. Perhaps a spell at No. 3 would unlock his strokes and even convince someone like Ian Chappell that he is an outstanding Test player.

The recall of Eddie Hemmings prompted quite a lot of discussion. We were hopeful that the Sydney wicket would respond to spin in the latter stages, but when we studied the statistics they showed that fast bowlers had captured more wickets at the SCG during the season than the spinners. Derek Pringle had bowled well in the victory in Melbourne and it was sad to drop a young player when his confidence was probably higher than it had been all tour. But Hemmings had bowled well against New South Wales and it was decided to go for him because this was a Test we had to win. Even a draw would be no good, and if we had the chance on a wearing wicket, an off-spinner might just swing things our way.

Despite the skipper's conviction that Australia would go for an outright victory rather than a largely defensive performance, I had my doubts, believing instead that unless we made the pace we could kiss the series and the Ashes goodbye. What we didn't need was the sort of umpiring decision which gave John Dyson a life in the opening over of the Australian innings. Greg Chappell had won the toss for the fourth time in the series, electing to bat first. Nearly forty thousand spectators were in position when Kepler Wessels played Bob Willis to mid-on and called Dyson for a sharp single which looked in doubt from the moment he set off. The skipper might not always look the most mobile cricketer around but on this occasion he responded brilliantly, picking up the ball and throwing down the stumps with Dyson out of his ground to our way of thinking. Our appeals for the run out were turned down by Mel Johnson who explained later that the margin was so close he had to give the benefit of the doubt to Dyson. 'I could only give it as I saw it. I knew it was six inches either way and because I wasn't sure I gave it to the batsman.' It's true, of course, that umpires can only decide on what they see and replays and pictures only fuel controversy over what has to be decided at the time. To us, though, Dyson looked a good foot short of his ground and even former Australian all-rounder Keith Miller, a man who doesn't pull his punches, wrote that Johnson's decision might have cost us the Ashes. In a back page article in the *Sydney Daily Telegraph* Miller argued: 'The controversial John Dyson incident comes on top of that shocking umpiring decision against David Gower in Melbourne. They were both glaring mistakes against England.'

It is always difficult to assess just how much umpiring decisions can affect the final outcome of a match. I would draw away from stating that the Dyson verdict cost us the chance of squaring the series and holding on to the Ashes. Dyson is not the stodgy player of old and the fact that he was still there at the end of the rain-interrupted first day didn't make it any easier for us when we watched the television highlights later that evening. If Dyson had gone in that first over, it would have put the Australians under the kind of pressure we had hoped to force on them. As it was, with the rain cutting more than two hours out of the day's play, and Dyson staying put through everything, we felt that our chances had slipped badly. I picked up the wicket of Wessels fairly cheaply and Chappell departed leg before to Bob Willis before Dyson and Hughes saw Australia through to 138 for 2 at the early close.

We desperately needed an early breakthrough at the start of the second day and Hughes, bless him, duly obliged with one of those rather fortunate wickets which have come my way from time to time. The ball was short and I swear I could see the sparkle in Hughes's eye as he prepared to pick his spot. I had seen him smash balls like that for 6 before but this time he pulled it low towards mid-on, where Cowans gratefully swooped to accept the chance. It was a very pleasant way to start the morning and it got better when Hookes failed to live up to the early promise he had shown against the spinners. I enjoy Hookes's batting: you always know that the storm might blow itself out at any time but while it's raging there's sure to be plenty worth applauding. I didn't feel much like cheering when he drove me to the boundary, but just when he seemed set for a major innings he contrived to get himself out, aiming to cut but instead edging to slip a ball which was too far up and too close to him. Once again we could congratulate ourselves that the roof hadn't fallen in.

Eventually Dyson became fifth man out after batting for more than 300 minutes. With Rod Marsh following him back to the pavilion soon after lunch we felt we were working ourselves back into the game, with Australia tottering on 219 for 6. Unfortunately, the form which Allan Border had been threatening all summer now arrived fully, to deny us the opportunity of wrapping up the innings quickly. Time was an important factor and when David Gower missed Border at silly point when he had made 15, Allan slowly built on the confidence gained from his innings at Melbourne to take Australia past 300 before he was last out late in the afternoon. I finished with 4 wickets in a spell of 30 overs and was pleased that I managed to get a fair amount of swing with the second new ball; it must have made Keith Miller happy too: he'd accused me of not swinging the ball a centimetre in Australia. Bob Willis delayed taking the new ball for 10 overs, a puzzling decision when Yardley, never happy against pace, was helping himself to runs against the spinners. Eddie Hemmings and Geoff Miller collected 4 wickets between them, a good sign for the chances of spin playing a decisive part later in the match, but first we had to get a formidable total on the board if they were going to get a decent opportunity in Australia's second innings.

Once again, though, the Australian fast bowlers put us under pressure from the start when Tavaré lost his off stump in the third over of the innings after lunging nervously at a very quick ball from Lawson. Cook, never happy, prodded forward uncertainly against Hogg and provided Chappell with yet one more catch at first slip. Then, disastrously, Lamb didn't offer a shot to the third delivery he faced from Lawson; when the ball seamed back he had no defence to offer as it glanced off his pads on to the stumps. We were 20-odd for 3. The Australians must have been wondering which day they would be opening the champagne to celebrate the return of the Ashes.

Derek Randall had other ideas and those still wondering just how much he had been affected mentally by the blow he had received from Holding were quickly given an answer. Naturally the Australians tested him out with several short-pitched deliveries but he refused to flinch. By the end of the second day we had managed to avoid any further disasters, thanks, also, to a flamboyant innings from David Gower. He and Randall maintained the tempo the following morning, steaming along at a run a minute with a marvellous mixture of unorthodox shots. They added 122 and for a time our nostrils were twitching again with the faint scent of an improbable victory.

Randall, I think, deserves a lot of praise for his performances on tour. He seems to have the ability to annoy the Australian players quicker than any other England batsman with his restless energy and constant 'rabbit', but he proved on this trip that he was worth his place in the middle order. (His batting in the one-day series grew even more outlandish, but few can doubt that there is a quality player fighting to come out from behind all those nervous mannerisms.) No-one would have thought any the less of him had he decided that the injury he received against Holding was still fresh enough in his mind to keep him out of the Sydney Test. Instead, on the third day, playing with Gower, he produced some of the most entertaining cricket of the series. He led the counter-attack much in the fashion of his famous Centenary Test 174 in Melbourne; one could sense that the mood out in the middle was changing as the Australian players started to feel the threat.

The Australian fast bowlers found their second wind to demolish our hopes: Randall got an inside edge on to his stumps while attempting to cut Thomson. My own contribution to our 237 first innings total was not impressive. I was dropped on 1 by Yardley, then went to Thomson when he got a ball to lift and it took my glove on the way to Wessels in the gully. We knew we should be taking full advantage of Randall's brave innings, yet by lunch we were struggling again when Gower was dismissed in the last over of the session. After holding himself in check all morning, he was suddenly tempted by Lawson's fifth ball, a half-volley; but the attempted drive looked a shade too hurried and Chappell took another incredible catch, diving a long way to his left at slip. It was a bad moment to lose a wicket. From then on Thomson conjured up some of his old fire to finish with 5 wickets and despite some spirited resistance from Miller and Hemmings we found ourselves trailing by 77 runs, 2 fewer than John Dyson's first innings score. That night our lingering feeling of injustice was heightened after Kim Hughes had been given not out in the last over of the day when Australia were wavering in their second innings. He played a ball on to his boot from where we believed it looped into the hands of Geoff Cook, diving to his left at short leg. Derek Randall was so sure of the validity of the catch that he ran from short cover to shake Cook's hand but after that it was only our heads which were shaking when umpire Dick French refused the appeals.

It was not an easy decision to give, because French first had to decide whether the ball touched Hughes's bat and, if it did, whether it touched the ground before being caught by Cook. French didn't think it was out, we did; and while that was fair enough things were not made any easier to bear when we heard on the grapevine that Hughes was saying he thought the catch was a fair one. Still, he wasn't the first batsman to remain at the wicket after getting the benefit of a doubtful decision, and he went on to play a crucial innings after the rest day.

We believed that Eddie Hemmings, and to some extent Geoff Miller, would hold the key to our chances of dismissing Australia cheaply enough to give ourselves a hope in the fourth innings. The wicket had been taking an increasing amount of turn and I tended to agree with the skipper when he thought that our odds were slightly longer than even – if, that is, we managed to restrict Australia to a lead of around 300. I spent the rest day on a yacht cruising round Sydney harbour and for a few very relaxing hours was able to think about the way the series had gone while gazing at possibly one of the finest views in the world – the Opera House and the Harbour Bridge. I finished off the day with a dozen of Sydney's finest rock oysters, believing I was mentally just right for the two days of hard labour ahead.

We certainly couldn't complain with the start we had on the fourth day when Hookes went cheaply to Miller, but from that point the Ashes were shifted inexorably from our grasp as Hughes and Border pulled Australia round with a partnership which drew the sting from the spinners on whom we had placed so much hope. Border began ominously by driving Miller for two 4s and then Hughes carted Hemmings for another couple to set the tempo for the partnership. The fifth-wicket pair put on 149 and it became increasingly evident that the series was being sewn up during their stand. Neither Eddie Hemmings nor Geoff Miller could dominate batting of such high quality. Both Hughes and Border used their feet superbly, dancing down the wicket like John Travolta; the off-spinners' confidence was being chipped away by one boundary after another.

I thought both off-spinners bowled too short, but I also have to say I don't suppose Border had batted with more authority at any time in the series. Hughes, too, was underlining the fact that, like David Gower, he had made the decisive step from being an unpredictable player into a batsman who would rub your nose into the dust given half a chance. He had tucked his impetuous image into his back pocket and found that a sense of responsibility did not put his talent into deep freeze. I was surprised to be told that Hughes hadn't previously reached fifty on the Sydney ground because he batted with such elegant assurance the place looked like his second home. You could tell the innings was giving him enormous pleasure; every boundary provided him with more ammunition to fire back at the critics who had held him responsible for England's triumph in the 1981 series.

The hundred partnership came up at almost a run a minute and when Hughes then went down the wicket to drive Hemmings for 6, our thoughts flipped back to the previous evening's controversial decision when we believed he'd been caught by Cook. It was no good worrying over what-might-have-been – by the time Border went for 83, the Ashes were as good as back in Australia, and Marsh's belligerent innings only reinforced our opinion that Chappell would not declare if it gave us even the remotest chance of forcing victory. In our own minds we believed that any target beyond 300 would give us problems. The screw turned unmercifully, with Hughes reaching 137 in a final Australian total of 382, a lead of 459.

As it turned out both Hemmings and Miller were expensive for the 6 wickets they shared in nearly 100 overs of combined toil. For me the day was a little cameo of the whole series: we had been at Australia's shoulder so many times yet only at Melbourne had we produced the sustained effort to pass them on the line. If I am totally honest, I must say that the overall standard of the series would not rank among the best of all time, yet at certain times during the five Tests individual performances were of the highest quality. Sadly for us, Australia had produced a few more of these magic moments than we had. It was happening now as at 113 for 4 in their second innings, Hughes and Border arrived with a partnership that slapped us down again, on this occasion for the very last time.

By stumps on the fourth day we had lost Geoff Cook cheaply, and although Eddie Hemmings produced a remarkable innings of 95 as nightwatchman there was never any real hope of pulling off a sensational win on the final day. Ten thousand were there to salute an Ashes victory but at least we denied them the sight of a total Test triumph by producing our best second innings display of the series. It wasn't much fun, though, knowing that we were playing only for pride; my series ended rather ironically when I was adjudged leg before to a ball which Thomson had angled across me from wide of the crease. When the finger went up I managed half a smile, half a shrug and trudged off, thinking that my Test runs – there were 270 of them in 10 innings – didn't adequately reflect the way I played when I was at the wicket. I never felt in bad nick but at the same time I wasn't able to put together an innings of prolonged quality. On too many occasions I threatened but couldn't quite deliver, and that was the difference between my performances on the tour and those against Australia in 1981. I guess it was time for the pendulum to swing the other way.

Our last-day total of 314 for 7 was built around Hemmings who batted for nearly four hours to deny Australia a victory which they never really deserved after their rather negative approach. Thomson had to bowl to me with the field spread deep and no slip, which seemed a shade conservative when only one team could win at that stage. Maybe Chappell had thought Kim Hughes was being serious the previous evening when he warned that I could walk on water. By now many other Australians must have felt there was lead in my boots. Obviously the Australian captain had not been reading Keith Miller's verdict that I was a shadow of a great all-rounder, or listening to Ian Chappell's televised boast that he was betting against me getting 350 runs in the series. That Mr Chappell and I have never seen eye to eye and I will be happy to accommodate any personal bets should he wish to gamble against me in the future. Brother Greg clearly didn't share Ian's lack of confidence in my batting ability, though by spreading the field both for myself and for Derek Randall, I thought he was taking caution too far. Greg had collected his critics in his forty-seven Tests as captain, but mostly his influence as a leader has been substantial . . . and as a batsman it has been stunning. To opponents his attitude is sometimes disdainful, sometimes perverse, but he has earned the hardcore support of the Australian team during recent seasons and that in itself has been no mean achievement. If he meant now to leave cricket, the game would be the poorer for it. Those who greeted his decision to stand down with pleasure placed too much emphasis, I think, on his period with World Series Cricket and his reluctance to tour abroad while his business interests were growing. This may have been annoying to some, yet while Chappell was absent no-one emerged to kick him off the throne.

The drawn game in Sydney which secured the Ashes for Australia left the England dressing-room with something akin to a *Marie Celeste* atmosphere. A few magazines were strewn around, a half-consumed plate of sandwiches was left on a chair. Then the press came to conduct a post mortem on the series with the skipper. Players who for the last few months had endured the special stresses of an Ashes series were now getting used to the fact that they had been lost, and for some it was a bitter experience. Everyone went to the victorious Australian dressing-room with words of congratulation, a hard duty for one or two. No-one likes to be part of a side which has surrendered the Ashes and each player had his own way of trying to ease the pain of failure in the pit of the stomach. My feelings were for Bob Willis, who would not get a chance to win the Ashes back, and for the younger players like Norman Cowans, Graeme Fowler and Derek Pringle denied the magnificent experience of an Ashes victory. But their turn will come, I'm sure. I spent the first hour or so after the match ended helping the Australians to consume their victory champagne and watching Jeff Thomson give a demonstration of his prawn-peeling prowess. Defeat troubled me as much as any other member of the England team, but I had joined the Australians at the end of play throughout the series and I saw no reason to hide myself away now.

I left the Sydney cricket ground that evening for dinner at my rented home with a journalist friend – and found myself involved in another controversial episode which I hadn't bargained for. We discussed a variety of things including my opinions on the umpiring during the series, but they were private views inasmuch as I didn't wish them to be published at that time. It had been made quite clear to every member of the party that all talk of umpires was strictly taboo and Bob Willis set the standard for this by keeping his lips tightly closed and suffering in silence like the rest of us. It was a fair enough policy: an outburst against decisions during the series would have inflamed feelings all round. Now the series was over I was prepared to discuss the England party's and my own unhappiness with a number of decisions. Unfortunately, due mostly to a misunderstanding, that discussion appeared in a newspaper and was speedily sent back on the wires to Australia where it appeared all over the front pages of certain other papers. The 'revelations' cost me a £200 fine and a rap from manager Doug Insole; it put the seal on a season of disappointment.

Perhaps the breathing space between the Melbourne and Sydney Tests was too short, perhaps the odds were always that the final Test would be anti-climax after such an effort. We didn't have the firepower to force victory once Chappell had won the toss and reversed the trend in the series by deciding to bat first. Apart from the upsetting Dyson run-out incident we were from the start struggling half a yard behind Australia and only threatened to catch them for a short period on the third day when Gower and Randall prospered for a glorious hour. Eddie Hemmings had waited all tour for a wicket which would offer him some help, and when the chance came he must have regretted that he couldn't make more of it: I'm sure he would have swapped his 95 runs in the second innings for a few more Australian wickets. But it would be unfair to criticize him when others, including I. T. Botham, had failed to make as much of an impact on the course of the game. Hughes duly accepted the Man of the Match award and Lawson stepped up to take the honours as Man of the Series, well deserved since he had given us trouble from the second innings at Perth and had bowled with increased aggression as his confidence improved. Chappell, with centuries at Perth and Adelaide, had promised to punish us from one end of Australia to another. If he didn't quite do that at least he had the satisfaction of regaining the Ashes and retiring from the Australian captaincy as a winner. I envied him the feeling.

7

Tested and Tried

WHEN I LOOK BACK in years to come at a Test series in which I managed only 270 runs in 10 innings, and 18 wickets at more than 40 apiece, I might come to the conclusion that I had endured a pretty miserable tour. But if I do, I hope also that I recall memories which go beyond those unimpressive figures to remind me that it wasn't quite the shambles some people now would have us believe. There were moments when things didn't go well, of course; there were times, even, when I might have disagreed with the tactics being employed to retain the Ashes. But while my own personal performances lacked the sparkle of previous summers I don't think the tour as a whole was a disaster. On balance it left me reasonably confident about the health of English cricket.

I began the tour thinking of one of my favourite proverbs:

> None sends his arrow to the mark in view
> Whose hand is feeble or his aim untrue.

I like to feel that I ended the tour with those sentiments still uppermost in my mind and that those who sought to put a damp blanket over my career as a Test all-rounder would find that there would be nothing feeble about my response to the predicament.

My performances on the field in Australia have never been first-rate. As a Whitbread scholar in Melbourne, a combination of poor weather and lack of form was responsible for my failure to make a resounding impression on my Australian hosts. Then, in 1978/9, on Mike Brearley's tour, I could hardly claim to have pulled up any trees, even though my 291 runs in 10 innings gave me third place in the Test batting averages behind

David Gower and Derek Randall, and I managed a commendable 23 wickets at 20-odd apiece. I felt before leaving on the latest tour, though, that the Australians hadn't seen the very best of Ian Botham competing in their own backyard, despite my innings of 119 in the third Test at Melbourne in 1980. Sadly, I still feel that I owe the Australians at home a big performance or two and hope I'll get the chance to provide them before I call it a day. Despite all the mocking messages on the posters around the Australian grounds, I feel there are a large number of supporters there who would love nothing more than to see me produce the goods and until I do that there will always be something missing in terms of personal satisfaction when I look back at my career. Still, it was good to hear manager Doug Insole come to my defence, arguing that other big-name players have had bad tours, notably Denis Compton in Australia in 1950/1 and Peter May in South Africa in 1956/7.

If I had to find a word to sum up my 1982/3 performance, I would go no higher than 'adequate', and I'm afraid that's nowhere near good enough, no matter what others might say. But, when I attempt to analyze my failure, especially with the bat, I can find no thread which links my Test dismissals together. The bounce was sometimes disconcerting, but there were so many occasions when I felt I was set for a big score that to blame the wicket for my eventual downfall would be grossly unfair. I sincerely believed that I was the victim of at least two debatable umpiring decisions but, having acknowledged that as an unfortunate by-product of the increased pressure on Test umpires, I wouldn't like to leave the impression that I'm blaming my lack of success on bad luck. I wouldn't seek that sort of excuse for myself nor for the team as a whole – it's my belief that with a little bit more class we would have overcome our misfortunes. As for fielding, I can hardly blame the light, since on Brearley's tour I snapped up 11 catches in the Tests, and even this time I pocketed another 9, several of which gave me a great deal of satisfaction. As a team, when the avalanche started to roll, there were times it seemed we didn't have enough belief in our own ability to see us to safety. You could pick out perhaps a dozen outstanding individual performances, but so often they were achieved in isolation and the concerted effort which we needed to shift the Australians off their perch rarely arrived.

Increasingly, my performance seemed to be made the focal point for all of England's troubles, and it was not easy to concentrate on getting my game right while worrying about the next story probing either my fitness, my attitude or my desire to win. I'm afraid poor Kathy and the rest of the family took the brunt of my frustration at not being able to produce the sort of performances which would have brought some succour to the team and some peace and quiet to the Botham household. I did feel that this was my worst overseas tour with the bat but, while I was no doubt a bit difficult to live with at the time, I didn't let it get me down for long. Just as I hope I don't let success go to my head, so I refuse to let failure gnaw away at my spirit. I never believe that a bad run will last forever, and I had as much confidence in my overall ability at the end of the tour as I had on the day it started. I will never have the total dedication of someone like Geoff Boycott, though, because I think there's more to life than twenty-two players batt- ling it out on a cricket pitch. I think I do put as much into my game as the next guy and that to subdue my spirits would only curb my effectiveness.

How many of the people who have had a go about my weight in past seasons could bowl twenty or thirty overs in the heat of Australia? There was nothing wrong with my stamina nor, for that matter, with my fitness. I was only really troubled by my back once on the tour and those who felt, like Bob Willis, that I had reached a crossroads in my career and needed to stand back and look at myself before deciding which way to turn, were wide of the mark. I believe I have two years left in me as a strike bowler in Test cricket and, without putting too fine a point on it, I wonder just who would replace me if I went earlier than that. Norman Cowans might make it, but his approach in the summers ahead will be crucial. The lack of quick bowlers in England has given Norman his chance very early on in his career and, while I feel he has lots of natural ability, he must now prove that he can work hard and show a will to continue. He came out to Australia very raw and still has a lot to learn, but just talking to people like Dennis Lillee and watching some of the Australian fast bowlers at close range can only have done him a world of good. It must have been pretty miserable for Norman early in the tour when he was learning one or two painful lessons about bowling in Test cricket, but his response in Melbourne, when he finally clutched the new ball in his hands, was surely a clue to his depth of character.

I'm optimistic that Cowans will emerge into the top bracket, just as I expect Derek Pringle to use his experience of the tour to sort out his Test future. Suggestions from some quarters that Derek is inclined to be lazy were perhaps provoked by his very relaxed attitude. I think he's got as much natural ability as any young cricketer in England, but now that he's no longer an 'unknown' from university he'll have to harden up cricket-wise and really get stuck into his game. He has enough ability to make him an England all-rounder for years to come, perhaps replacing one Ian Botham when it is finally decided that I've done enough hard labour in the England attack.

It wasn't easy for Bob Willis to lead a side which depended to a fairly large extent on untried talent, and I certainly wouldn't be among those who jumped up to criticize him at the end of it. When Bob was appointed the selectors knew they weren't getting a master tactician like Mike Brearley, so I feel no-one should be disappointed on that score. The criticisms that he handled Cowans badly in the early part of the tour quite ignored another school of thought that, by holding Norman back, Willis ensured that he would make a more telling contribution later on. The other major criticism, that he played Allan Border back into form and almost lost another Test with his tactics at Melbourne, was similarly unfounded, in my view. If a captain believes that what he is doing is right, he should not be swayed by others, even when his theories are taken to the brink, as they were on the final day of the marvellous Melbourne Test. If Bob had faltered, or switched tactics to attack Border as well as Thomson, who is to say that we would have won? I would prefer to remember that we had the privilege of taking part in one of the most thrilling Tests of all time and that the justification of the tactics came in the moment when Geoff Miller clutched the catch which won us the game.

I think Bob's greatest triumph on a long and difficult tour was that he kept the party in harmony even when results weren't good. Everybody stuck together, there were no hang-ups, no punch-ups. Rumours of a rift between the captain and myself were pure moonshine, and I'm happy to put that on record. This tour party could justifiably have been faulted on some points, but the way in which the players worked for each other was a tribute to the perseverance, patience and cool humour of the captain, assisted in no small way by the manager. I won't easily forget that when the Ashes had finally gone on the last day at Sydney, Bob waited out on the pitch to shake the hand of every Australian player as they came off for their celebrations. At that moment he must have been feeling all the frustra-tions of the previous three months, the hurt of losing and the worry of not knowing whether he had just played in his last Test as captain. Yet he still wanted to be the first to offer a hand of congratulation to the winners.

Bob knew there were limitations to the ability of the side from the outset, but on a long tour you always hope that players picked for their potential can come through and prove decisive. Graeme Fowler was a case in point, after scoring runs in his only previous Test match and arriving in Australia with so little experience. I suppose it was to be expected that he made a nightmare start but then, just when he appeared ready to score a few runs and justify the faith of the selectors, he injured his toe and missed the final Test. Nevertheless, I think he had already shown he was a gutsy little fighter who wanted to prove to a few people, and most especially the Australian fast bowlers, that he had it in him to make a Test cricketer. Certainly, I won't forget Graeme's performance on the field in a hurry: he might be a great fielder, sure enough, but I reckon he's got the worst underarm throw back to a bowler of anyone I know in cricket!

While Fowler took time to settle, and Geoff Cook fought to find the right technique on Australian wickets, the real surprise of the tour didn't emerge until the closing stages. Of all the untried players, reserve wicketkeeper Ian Gould was a tonic off the pitch and a terror on it when he got the chance. He sat on his behind for a large part of the Test tour, but kept superbly fit thanks to his tireless work in the nets. On some days, he had nothing more arduous to do than to walk out with the drinks trolley. But, when spirits needed to be lifted, Ian was always ready with a joke or two. And, when the chance came, as it did when he fielded as substitute for Graeme Fowler at Melbourne, he grabbed his opportunity with stunning agility. I liked the look of him, too, in the one-day internationals; and for those who believed that standing back to Imran Khan and Garth Le Roux at Sussex had blunted his edge against the spinners, I can only say that, in my opinion, he had no problems with Vic Marks and Geoff Miller. I think the experience of the tour benefitted him enormously and I can think of no higher praise than to say that he looked like an England Test wicketkeeper to me.

Among the more experienced players, Gower was the quality batsman of the series, more often than not coming in to face the flak when the openers had failed. The real test of a great player is to score runs consistently when others are struggling, and so often in the series Gower prospered on those occasions when the Australian quick bowlers had their tails up. I felt his influence as vice-captain grew in stature as the tour progressed, but I hope the powers-that-be think carefully before giving him the skipper's job on a full-time basis: I would hate to see another fine talent sacrificed in the quest for a fresh captain and time, after all, is still on David's side. Allan Lamb did everything that was expected of him and promised even more for the future; while Derek Randall, at times audacious, at times exasperating, proved just how much of a toughie lurks behind the joker's mask.

The major disappointment of the tour, apart from my own wretched form with the bat, was almost certainly our performance at Adelaide, where we should have saved the Test. To some it appeared a pretty spineless performance; my own feeling was that the problems we knew we had with the side – namely, at the top of the order and with our strike bowling support – were exposed sufficiently for Australia to inflict a telling defeat. I hate losing, especially to Australia, and when a game is given away on a plate the feeling of disgust haunts me for days afterwards. The critics, almost to a man, found Willis guilty, but he had my support at the time and I wouldn't abandon him now, especially remembering that it was partly the force of my own argument which persuaded him to put Australia in to bat in Adelaide.

I felt Willis was let down by his players and my only criticism of his captaincy was that he tended to be too defensive. I felt there were a number of times when he opted for a negative line when my own instincts were telling me to attack. I recall his field placing at Perth when Greg Chappell came in to bat and was not pressurised sufficiently, when we all knew he was susceptible to the short-pitched delivery. I tend to be too ambitious in my thinking, wanting to over-attack, to solve a particular crisis by blasting away at the opposition. Bob goes the other way – I suppose if you drew a line down the middle, you'd get somewhere near the right approach.

If I had one other criticism of the tour it was that it lasted much too long. The first couple of months were magnificent, but after that people started thinking about all the things they were missing back home. In my case it was a pint with my mates in the local on Sunday morning, and long walks with my pet boxer, Tigger. I've had one Christmas at home in the last seven years – and that was a disaster because not only did I catch pneumonia but the police decided to choose Christmas Eve to serve me with a summons. I hope the cricket authorities might think of ways to regulate these demanding tours differently, otherwise the last few matches can become a drudge. New Zealand triumphed in the one-day internationals partly for this reason, and I can't believe they will ever catch us like that again.

In hindsight it's always easier to look at the overall tactics of the tour and wonder whether we got them right. Should we have steamed into the first Test in Perth and risked going one down so early in the tour? When I bowled badly in Brisbane, did the skipper lose patience and allow his overall planning to appear haphazard? Should we have batted first at Adelaide where Australia managed well over 400 after being sent in? In many ways it was a strange tour, because at the end of it we felt we had almost done well. The difference between the two teams was minimal and, considering the fact that when we left England we were regarded as no-hopers, the final series score of 2–1 couldn't be called a disaster. There is always a fine line between success and failure. And for the players who took part in the fourth Test victory, there will always be the memory of the drama on that last day at Melbourne. For some, it will be that memory which outlasts all others at the end of their careers.

The tour started with talk about my fitness and it finished in pretty much the same way, with several people close to me jumping aboard the bandwagon. I found the whole thing amusing. Why is it that just because I have a mediocre tour people have to invent reasons for it? Why can't they accept that I'm human? I didn't make excuses for myself and didn't need other people to make them on my behalf. My only real injury on tour was in a one-day game at Melbourne, when I pulled a muscle in my side and didn't want to bowl in the next match at Adelaide. In the end I was persuaded to do so but when New Zealand scored 290-odd to win I wished I hadn't been so compliant.

My training schedule hasn't altered in the last seven years and my weight, when I ended the tour, was the same as it was two years before. I couldn't understand why so many people wanted to analyse my performances and leave almost everyone else on tour alone. Being constantly probed about fitness and attitude doesn't make the business of recapturing my best form any easier.

I'll be back, don't worry. And maybe, too, I'll be able to enjoy a pint in peace without all the part-time Dr Kildares rushing for the weight charts. I'll look forward to the peace and quiet, believe me.

Test Scores
and Averages

Australia *v.* England: FIRST TEST
Perth, 12, 13, 14, 16, 17 November 1982

ENGLAND

	First Innings			Second Innings	
G. Cook	c Dyson, b Lillee	1 – (2)		c Border, b Lawson	7
C. J. Tavaré	c Hughes, b Yardley	89 – (1)		c Chappell, b Yardley	9
D. I. Gower	c Dyson, b Alderman	72 –		lbw, b Lillee	28
A. J. Lamb	c Marsh, b Yardley	46 –		c Marsh, b Lawson	56
I. T. Botham	c Marsh, b Lawson	12 –		b Lawson	0
D. W. Randall	c Wood, b Yardley	78 –		b Lawson	115
G. Miller	c Marsh, b Lillee	30 – (8)		c Marsh, b Yardley	0
D. R. Pringle	b Lillee	0 – (9)		not out	47
R. W. Taylor	not out	29 – (7)		b Yardley	31
R. G. D. Willis	c Lillee, b Yardley	26 –		b Lawson	0
N. G. Cowans	b Yardley	4 –		lbw, b Chappell	36
Extras	(b7, lb9, w2, nb6)	24		(b5, lb11, w2, nb11)	29
TOTAL	(155.4 overs)	411		(116.3 overs)	358

Fall of Wickets: 1–14, 2–109, 3–189, 4–204, 5–304, 6–323, 7–342, 8–357, 9–406
Second Innings: 1–10, 2–51, 3–77, 4–80, 5–151, 6–228, 7–242, 8–292, 9–292

AUSTRALIA BOWLING

	O	M	R	W	O	M	R	W
Lillee	38	13	96	3	33	12	89	1
Alderman	43	15	84	1				
Lawson	29	6	89	1	32	5	108	5
Chappell	3	0	11	0	2.3	1	8	1
Yardley	42.4	15	107	5	41	10	101	3
Border					7	2	21	0
Hookes					1	0	2	0

Australia *v.* England: FIRST TEST
Perth, 12, 13, 14, 16, 17 November 1982

AUSTRALIA

	First Innings			Second Innings	
G. M. Wood	c & b Willis	29	–	c Taylor, b Willis	0
J. Dyson	lbw, b Miller	52	–	c Cowans, b Willis	12
A. R. Border	c Taylor, b Botham	8	–	not out	32
G. S. Chappell	c Lamb, b Willis	117	–	not out	22
K. J. Hughes	c Willis, b Miller	62			
D. W. Hookes	lbw, b Miller	56			
R. W. Marsh	c Cook, b Botham	0			
G. F. Lawson	b Miller	50			
B. Yardley	c Lamb, b Willis	17			
D. K. Lillee	not out	2			
Extras	(b4, lb1, w1, nb25)	31		(lb1, nb6)	7
TOTAL	(for 9 dec; 131.5 overs)	424		(2 wkts; 22 overs)	73

Fall of Wickets: 1–63, 2–76, 3–123, 4–264, 5–311, 6–311, 7–374, 8–414, 9–424
Second Innings: 1–2, 2–22

ENGLAND BOWLING

	O	M	R	W	O	M	R	W
Willis	31.5	4	95	3	6	1	23	2
Botham	40	10	121	2	6	1	17	0
Cowans	13	2	54	0	3	1	15	0
Pringle	10	1	37	0	2	0	3	0
Miller	33	11	70	4	4	3	8	0
Cook	4	2	16	0				
Lamb					1	1	0	0

MATCH DRAWN

Umpires: A. R. Crafter and M. W. Johnson
Man of the Match: D. W. Randall

Australia *v.* England: SECOND TEST
Brisbane, 26, 27, 28, 30 November, 1 December 1982

ENGLAND:

	First Innings		Second Innings	
C. J. Tavaré	c Hughes, b Lawson	1 –	c Marsh, b Lawson	13
G. Fowler	c Yardley, b Lawson	7 –	c Marsh, b Thomson	83
D. I. Gower	c Wessels, b Lawson	18 –	c Marsh, b Thomson	34
A. J. Lamb	c Marsh, b Lawson	72 –	c Wessels, b Thomson	12
I. T. Botham	c Rackemann, b Yardley	40 – (6)	c Marsh, b Thomson	15
D. W. Randall	c Lawson, b Rackemann	37 – (5)	c Yardley, b Thomson	4
G. Miller	c Marsh, b Lawson	0 –	c Marsh, b Lawson	60
R. W. Taylor	c Lawson, b Rackemann	1 –	c Hookes, b Lawson	3
E. E. Hemmings	not out	15 –	b Lawson	18
R. G. D. Willis	c Thomson, b Yardley	1 –	not out	10
N. G. Cowans	c Marsh, b Lawson	10 –	c Marsh, b Lawson	5
Extras	(lb2, w1, nb14)	17	(b8, lb8, w1, nb35)	52
TOTAL	(64.3 overs)	219	(127.3 overs)	309

Fall of Wickets: 1–8, 2–13, 3–63, 4–141, 5–152, 6–152, 7–178, 8–191, 9–195
Second Innings: 1–54, 2–144, 3–165, 4–169, 5–194, 6–201, 7–226, 8–285, 9–295

AUSTRALIA BOWLING

	O	M	R	W	O	M	R	W
Lawson	18.3	4	47	6	35.3	11	87	5
Rackemann	21	8	61	2	12.2	3	35	0
Thomson	8	0	43	0	31	6	73	5
Yardley	17	5	51	2	40.4	21	50	0
Chappell					6	2	8	0
Hookes					2	0	4	0

Australia *v.* England: SECOND TEST
Brisbane, 26, 27, 28, 30 November, 1 December 1982

AUSTRALIA:

	First Innings		Second Innings	
K. Wessels	b Willis	162 –	b Hemmings	46
J. Dyson	b Botham	1 –	retired hurt	4
A. R. Border	c Randall, b Willis	0 –	c Botham, b Hemmings	15
G. S. Chappell	run out	53 –	c Lamb, b Cowans	8
K. J. Hughes	c Taylor, b Botham	0 –	not out	39
D. W. Hookes	c Taylor, b Miller	28 –	not out	66
R. W. Marsh	c Taylor, b Botham	11		
B. Yardley	c Tavaré, b Willis	53		
G. F. Lawson	c Hemmings, b Willis	6		
C. G. Rackemann	b Willis	4		
J. R. Thomson	not out	5		
Extras	(b2, lb8, nb8)	18	(b2, lb5, nb5)	12
TOTAL	(110.4 overs)	341	(3 wkts; 60.5 overs)	190

Fall of Wickets: 1–4, 2–11, 3–94, 4–99, 5–130, 6–171, 7–271, 8–310, 9–332
Second Innings: 1–60, 2–77, 3–83

ENGLAND BOWLING

	O	M	R	W	O	M	R	W
Willis	29.4	3	66	5	4	1	24	0
Botham	22	1	105	3	15.5	1	70	0
Cowans	6	0	36	0	9	1	31	1
Hemmings	33.3	6	81	0	29	9	48	2
Miller	19.3	4	35	1	3	0	10	0

AUSTRALIA WON BY 7 WICKETS
Umpires: R. C. Bailhache and M. W. Johnson
Man of the Match: K. C. Wessels

Australia *v.* England: THIRD TEST
Adelaide, 10, 11, 12, 14, 15 December 1982

AUSTRALIA:

	First Innings			Second Innings	
K. C. Wessels	c Taylor, b Botham	44 – (2)	c Taylor, b Botham	1
J. Dyson	c Taylor, b Botham	44 – (1)	not out	37
G. S. Chappell	c Gower, b Willis	115 – (4)	not out	26
K. J. Hughes	run out	88		
G. Lawson	c Botham, b Willis	2 – (3)	c Randall, b Willis	14
A. R. Border	c Taylor, b Pringle	26		
D. W. Hookes	c Botham, b Hemmings	37		
R. W. Marsh	c Hemmings, b Pringle	3		
B. Yardley	c Gower, b Botham	38		
R. M. Hogg	not out	14		
J. R. Thomson	c & b Botham	3		
Extras	(lb6, nb18)	24	(nb5)	5
TOTAL	(156.5 overs)	438	(2 wkts; 23.5 overs)	83

Fall of Wickets: 1–76, 2–138, 3–264, 4–270, 5–315, 6–355, 7–359, 8–391, 9–430
Second Innings: 1–3, 2–37

ENGLAND BOWLING

	O	M	R	W	O	M	R	W
Willis	25	8	76	2	8	1	17	1
Botham	36.5	5	112	4	10	2	45	1
Pringle	33	5	97	2	1.5	0	11	0
Miller	14	2	33	0				
Hemmings	48	17	96	1	4	1	5	0

Australia *v.* England: THIRD TEST
Adelaide, 10, 11, 12, 14, 15 December 1982

ENGLAND:

	First Innings		Second Innings	
C. J. Tavaré	c Marsh, b Hogg	1 –	c Wessels, b Thomson	0
G. Fowler	c Marsh, b Lawson	11 –	c Marsh, b Lawson	37
D. I. Gower	c Marsh, b Lawson	60 –	b Hogg	114
A. J. Lamb	c Marsh, b Lawson	82 –	c Chappell, b Yardley	8
I. T. Botham	c Wessels, b Thomson	35 –	c Dyson, b Yardley	58
D. W. Randall	b Lawson	0 –	c Marsh, b Lawson	17
G. Miller	c Yardley, b Hogg	7 –	lbw, b Lawson	17
R. W. Taylor	c Chappell, b Yardley	2 – (9)	not out	3
D. R. Pringle	not out	1 – (8)	c Marsh, b Thomson	9
E. E. Hemmings	b Thomson	0 –	c Wessels, b Lawson	0
R. G. D. Willis	b Thomson	1 –	c Marsh, b Lawson	10
Extras	(lb5, nb11)	16	(b7, lb6, w3, nb15)	31
TOTAL	(67.4 overs)	216	(104 overs)	304

Fall of Wickets: 1–1, 2–21, 3–140, 4–181, 5–181, 6–194, 7–199, 8–213, 9–213
Second Innings: 1–11, 2–90, 3–118, 4–236, 5–247, 6–272, 7–277, 8–289, 9–290

AUSTRALIA BOWLING

	O	M	R	W	O	M	R	W
Lawson	18	4	56	4	24	6	66	5
Hogg	14	2	41	2	19	5	53	1
Thomson	14.5	3	51	3	13	3	41	2
Yardley	21	7	52	1	37	12	90	2
Border					8	2	14	0
Hookes					3	1	9	0

AUSTRALIA WON BY 8 WICKETS
Umpires: M. W. Johnson and R. A. French
Man of the Match: G. F. Lawson

Australia *v.* England: FOURTH TEST
Melbourne, 26, 27, 28, 29, 30 December 1982

ENGLAND:

	First Innings		Second Innings	
G. Cook	c Chappell, b Thomson	10 –	c Yardley, b Thomson	26
G. Fowler	c Chappell, b Hogg	4 –	b Hogg	65
C. J. Tavaré	c Yardley, b Thomson	89 –	b Hogg	0
D. I. Gower	c Marsh, b Hogg	18 –	c Marsh, b Lawson	3
A. J. Lamb	c Dyson, b Yardley	83 –	c Marsh, b Hogg	26
I. T. Botham	c Wessels, b Yardley	27 –	c Chappell, b Thomson	46
G. Miller	c Border, b Yardley	10 –	lbw, b Lawson	14
D. R. Pringle	c Wessels, b Hogg	9 –	c Marsh, b Lawson	42
R. W. Taylor	c Marsh, b Yardley	1 –	lbw, b Thomson	37
R. G. D. Willis	not out	6 –	not out	8
N. G. Cowans	c Lawson, b Hogg	3 –	b Lawson	10
Extras	(b3, lb6, w3, nb12)	24	(b2, lb9, nb6)	17
TOTAL	(81.3 overs)	284	(80.4 overs)	294

Fall of Wickets: 1–11, 2–25, 3–56, 4–217, 5–227, 6–259, 7–262, 8–268, 9–278
Second Innings: 1–40, 2–41, 3–45, 4–128, 5–129, 6–160, 7–201, 8–262, 9–280

AUSTRALIA BOWLING

	O	M	R	W	O	M	R	W
Lawson	17	6	48	0	21.4	6	66	4
Hogg	23.3	6	69	4	22	5	64	3
Yardley	27	9	89	4	15	2	67	0
Thomson	13	2	49	2	21	3	74	3
Chappell	1	0	5	0	1	0	6	0

Australia v. England: FOURTH TEST
Melbourne, 26, 27, 28, 29, 30 December 1982

AUSTRALIA:

	First Innings		Second Innings	
K. C. Wessels	b Willis	47 –	b Cowans	14
J. Dyson	lbw, b Cowans	21 –	c Tavaré, b Botham	31
G. S. Chappell	c Lamb, b Cowans	0 –	c sub (Gould), b Cowans	2
K. J. Hughes	b Willis	66 –	c Taylor, b Miller	48
A. R. Border	b Botham	2 – (6)	not out	62
D. W. Hookes	c Taylor, b Pringle	53 – (5)	c Willis, b Cowans	68
R. W. Marsh	b Willis	53 –	lbw, b Cowans	13
B. Yardley	b Miller	9 –	b Cowans	0
G. F. Lawson	c Fowler, b Miller	0 –	c Cowans, b Pringle	7
R. M. Hogg	not out	8 –	lbw, b Cowans	4
J. R. Thomson	b Miller	1 –	c Miller, b Botham	21
Extras	(lb8, nb19)	27	(b5, lb9, w1, nb3)	18
TOTAL	(79 overs)	287	(96.1 overs)	288

Fall of Wickets: 1–55, 2–55, 3–83, 4–89, 5–180, 6–261, 7–276, 8–276, 9–278
Second Innings: 1–37, 2–39, 3–71, 4–171, 5–173, 6–190, 7–190, 8–209, 9–218

ENGLAND BOWLING

	O	M	R	W	O	M	R	W
Willis	15	2	38	3	17	0	57	0
Botham	18	3	69	1	25.1	4	80	2
Cowans	16	0	69	2	26	6	77	6
Pringle	15	2	40	1	12	4	26	1
Miller	15	5	44	3	16	6	30	1

ENGLAND WON BY 3 RUNS
Umpires: R. W. Whitehead and A. R. Crafter
Man of the Match: N. G. Cowans

Australia *v*. England: FIFTH TEST
Sydney, 2, 3, 4, 6, 7 January 1983

AUSTRALIA:

	First Innings			Second Innings	
K. C. Wessels	c Willis, b Botham	19	– (2)	lbw, b Botham	53
J. Dyson	c Taylor, b Hemmings	79	– (1)	c Gower, b Willis	2
G. S. Chappell	lbw, b Willis	35	–	c Randall, b Hemmings	11
R. J. Hughes	c Cowans, b Botham	29	–	c Botham, b Hemmings	137
D. W. Hookes	c Botham, b Hemmings	17	–	lbw, b Miller	19
A. R. Border	c Miller, b Hemmings	89	–	c Botham, b Cowans	83
R. W. Marsh	c & b Miller	3	–	c Taylor, b Miller	41
B. Yardley	b Cowans	24	–	c Botham, b Hemmings	0
G. F. Lawson	c & b Botham	6	–	not out	13
J. R. Thomson	c Lamb, b Botham	0	–	c Gower, b Miller	12
R. M. Hogg	not out	0	–	run out	0
Extras	(b3, lb8, w2)	13		(lb7, nb4)	11
TOTAL	(115 overs)	314		(131.3 overs)	382

Fall of Wickets: 1–39, 2–96, 3–150, 4–173, 5–210, 6–219, 7–262, 8–283, 9–291
Second Innings: 1–23, 2–38, 3–82, 4–113, 5–262, 6–350, 7–357, 8–358, 9–382

ENGLAND BOWLING

	O	M	R	W	O	M	R	W
Willis	20	6	57	1	10	2	33	1
Cowans	21	3	67	1	13	1	47	1
Botham	30	8	75	4	10	0	35	1
Hemmings	27	10	68	3	47	16	116	3
Miller	17	7	34	1	49.3	12	133	3
Cook					2	1	7	0

Australia *v.* England: FIFTH TEST
Sydney, 2, 3, 4, 6, 7 January 1983

ENGLAND:

	First Innings		Second Innings	
G. Cook	c Chappell, b Hogg	8 –	lbw, b Lawson	2
C. J. Tavaré	b Lawson	0 –	lbw, b Yardley	16
D. I. Gower	c Chappell, b Lawson	70 – (4)	c Hookes, b Yardley	24
A. J. Lamb	b Lawson	0 – (5)	c & b Yardley	29
D. W. Randall	b Thomson	70 – (6)	b Thomson	44
I. T. Botham	c Wessels, b Thomson	5 – (7)	lbw, b Thomson	32
G. Miller	lbw, b Thomson	34 – (8)	not out	21
R. W. Taylor	lbw, b Thomson	0 – (9)	not out	28
E. E. Hemmings	c Border, b Yardley	29 (3)	c March, b Yardley	95
R. G. D. Willis	c Border, b Thomson	1	.	
N. G. Cowans	not out	0		
Extras	(b4, lb4, nb12)	20	(b1, lb10, w1, nb11) 23	
TOTAL	(64.5 overs)	237	(7 wkts; 96 overs)	314

Fall of Wickets: 1–8, 2–23, 3–24, 4–146, 5–163, 6–169, 7–170, 8–220, 9–232
Second Innings: 1–3, 2–55, 3–104, 4–155, 5–196, 6–260, 7–261, 8–314

AUSTRALIA BOWLING

	O	M	R	W	O	M	R	W
Lawson	20	2	70	3	15	1	50	1
Hogg	16	2	50	1	13	6	25	0
Thomson	14.5	2	50	5	12	3	30	2
Yardley	14	4	47	1	37	6	139	4
Border					16	3	36	0
Chappell					1	0	6	0
Hookes					2	1	5	0

MATCH DRAWN
Umpires: M. W. Johnson and R. A. French
Man of the Match: K. J. Hughes